ALZHEIMERS,

A Caregivers Journey

into LOVE

CAMERON

iUniverse books may be ordered through booksellers or by contacting:

iUniverse
1663 Liberty Drive
Bloomington, IN 47403
www.iuniverse.com
844-349-9409

Because of the dynamic nature of the Internet, any web addresses or links contained in this book may have changed since publication and may no longer be valid. The views expressed in this work are solely those of the author and do not necessarily reflect the views of the publisher, and the publisher hereby disclaims any responsibility for them.

ISBN: 978-1-6632-6408-4 (sc)
ISBN: 978-1-6632-6407-7 (e)

Library of Congress Control Number: 2024912255

Print information available on the last page.

iUniverse rev. date: 08/02/2024

ALZHEIMER'S

A CAREGIVER'S JOURNEY INTO LOVE

Dedicated

To

Donna Dean Haney

Introduction to: Alzheimer's- A Love Story

Okay, so you might ask yourself, "why do we need another book on Alzheimer's Disease?" I asked myself the same question. And my first response was, we don't. But that was years ago after my wife had been diagnosed with Alzheimer's. And I've learned over the years that that was really just my form of denial. I didn't want to journal my experiences, relive the horror of a perfectly healthy woman aged 56 being diagnosed with Alzheimer's disease. I thought that was just for 'old people'.

My name is Cameron Haney and as anyone who has had a spouse with this diagnosis knows, it's not just the spouse who receives this devastating sentence, it's both of us. And here begins a love story that truly tests the agreement, 'through sickness and health, till death do us part'. Well did I say it begins here, no it began on June 24th, 1982.

So why do we need another book on Alzheimer's, and what qualifies me to write it? I guess you'll have to read it to discover my qualifications. But the 'why' is simple, I do it to honor the most beautiful and honorable woman I've ever known. Come walk with me on a journey that will make you laugh and make you cry. And I hope will help you discover that you too can find love and hope, even in the midst of what at times is pure insanity!

Peace be with you, Cameron

Acknowledgements

I would like to give special thanks to Lifecoach Troy Troutman for his encouragement, as well as his many hours of editing and typing the manuscript, to get it ready to send it to the publisher. All of which he did voluntarily.

Equally many thanks to my better half, Denise, whose encouragement and also financial support have allowed me to go to the next level in my journey.

As well, my thanks to God for this opportunity to serve others through this book.

HUMILITY

Lord, how worthless am I to you?
For there is nothing that I can do
To please you at all with any pure deed
But yet I know they saw you bleed.

I cannot even; a blessing send
Lest it be for myself, always, in the end
For your kingdom is dangling for us to pay heed
But yet I know they saw you bleed.

Were it not for your grace,
Lord, that's so freely rendered
I doubt if we could have ever surrendered
So humbled, I stand here with all my need
But yet I know they saw you bleed.

So now you bless me and fill me with joy
And all feelings of worthlessness, you shall destroy
For I shall be filled with you so complete
Your power shall conquer all the trials that I meet.

Let us give you the glory for all that is good
Let us praise your name in all that we should
Dear Jesus, our strength and our victory, indeed
Bless your name evermore, for I saw you bleed.

Written by Donna

CHAPTER 1

In the Beginning

Donna was 34, and I was 29, when we married in that one-bedroom house in Anaheim, California. I remember calling my stepmom and asking if she was sitting down. She braced herself for whatever news I might have, not knowing if I was in jail or in the hospital or what. Mom seemed pleased when I told her I married Donna, whom she had yet to meet, and that she was 34. She and Dad figured she might bring some maturity to the marriage since she was older. Donna's parents were pleased as well. They were happy Donna finally found someone to spend her life with.

Donna and I were married on June 24, 1982, just two weeks after we had gone out on our first date. We had met through a mutual friend who happened to be in the same medical clinic as Donna. My friend Jane kept saying, "You need to meet this girl. She believes in God in the same way you do." And she would tell Donna, "You need to meet this guy. He believes in God in the same way you do." She arranged the meeting, so I met Donna at the clinic. I wasn't immediately stricken with this fair maiden. I found out later that her wide-eyed look was due to the meds she was taking. Nevertheless, two months later, we went out on a date.

Donna had been released from the clinic once her medicine had been regulated, for the manic depression she had discovered she had. It was a beautiful night in Southern California; we doubled with my friend Jane and her boyfriend, Bud. After a delicious dinner, we returned to Jane's house to talk. We all gabbed until the wee hours of the morning. Around 4 a.m., Donna and I left Jane's apartment. While standing out on the street, we decided we didn't want this romantic evening to end.

The weather was warm, and the quiet breeze was calm on the skin as we walked along the empty beach. Huntington Beach, California, is usually full of sunbathers and surfers during June, but not at four in the morning. We walked and talked until the sun came up, sharing each other's thoughts on God and life. Afterward, we drove back to our friend Jane's to pick up Donna's car. We decided I'd follow Donna to her rental house in Anaheim, about 15 miles from Stanton, where we were. Again, we didn't want to leave each other, so I crashed on the couch, and Donna went to bed. We were together day and night from then on. We both felt that it was Divine Providence that we were brought together. Even though most people usually had a long engagement period, we thought, why wait if it's God's will? I asked her to marry me after three days together. I don't know whether she had lost her mind or what, but she said "Yes." We discussed it and decided to go to Las Vegas and get married in one of the chapels there.

There was nothing but excitement in the air as we got in the car to drive to Los Angeles Airport. We had been together six or seven days by then and were flying on 'cloud nine.' Of course, we needed wedding rings. Luckily, Sears in Buena Park was on the way to L.A. We stopped, picked out two inexpensive rings quickly, and then went down the 91 Freeway to the airport. The airport was approximately 20 miles from Buena Park, and we wasted no time getting there. Arriving in record time, we drove to the overnight parking lot and parked the car. Walking as swiftly as we could, with no baggage or common sense, like two kids in a fairy tale, we bought our plane tickets at the ticket counter for Las Vegas, and then we sat down to wait. It was then we had our first "wake-up" call. We didn't have enough money for a hotel room and a chapel wedding. Oh, that was alright; we'd get married and return home. Then, "wake-up" call number two. While sitting there, still excited, I searched my pockets to ensure we had the rings I bought. To my shock and dismay, Donna's ring was missing. "How was that possible?" We drove straight from Sears to the airport. Even though it was around 7 p.m., we didn't care about stopping to eat, and we just wanted to get there as fast as possible. Where, where could I have lost the ring!"

It was then that the two kids snapped to and regained their adult senses. With heads down, we went to the ticket agent and turned in our plane tickets. Donna and I searched the car like a crime scene; the ring was the only evidence. Nowhere could it be found, but how, how could it be gone? Where else had I stopped? I mean, we didn't even stop to use the restroom. Then it hit me: the parking ticket. I had to get out of the car to grab the parking ticket. I ran full speed to where we entered the parking lot. There it was, lying on the ground right where it had fallen. Elated, I reached down and picked it up, only to realize what I had done. Her ring, a simple blank leading to three strands joined together at the top, had been flattened when the car tire ran it over. What had started as one of the most romantic adventures we'd remember ended up being one of the most foolish nights we'd probably rather forget. Our dream had become a nightmare. Well, it wasn't all that bad. The next day, we took the ring to my future father-in-law, who was skilled with his hands, and he fixed the ring back to almost like new. Not to be defeated, and still not changing our minds, we regrouped and went to plan B; of course, plan A and plan B we just made up as we went along, but it still worked out. We married at the county clerk's office in Santa Ana a week later.

Donna's parents were very gracious and gave us enough money for a honeymoon, which was much more exciting than the failed trip to Las Vegas.

At the time, my sister Lynne and her husband Vern lived in Roseburg, Oregon. We decided to take the AMTRAK train up the California coast to Oregon. When we reached the border, the train went inland through Grants Pass and then north to Roseburg. I hadn't seen my sister in a long time, and it gave us somewhere to go that wouldn't require us to pay for a hotel. The scenery along the coast of California is very beautiful. Equally spectacular were the forest and mountains of Oregon. Amtrak had those train cars full of windows, and we were seated high enough to see the beach at some spots.

When we arrived in Roseburg, Lynne and Vern had a surprise that made our honeymoon unique and unforgettable. Roseburg is a logging town, but Donna and I didn't know. Imagine our surprise when Vern drove us three miles up a mountain on a logging road with a sleeping bag and food and dropped us off. He instructed that he'd pick us up at the bottom of the mountain in three days. This was the end of June; the weather was great for hiking down a hill. It was a great place to be for two people who lived in the city. It was unbelievable to be in the forested mountains of Oregon, and to make things even better; we found a pond off the road hidden in the trees. We spent a few hours swimming and cooling off in the afternoon sun. It was the second day of an outdoor excursion that was peaceful and quiet until we felt the ground begin to tremble. You must understand we were from California. We'd both experienced earthquakes before, but we sure didn't expect to be in the middle of one in the forest of Oregon. It was then we felt the moving earthquake. We ran as fast as possible to get off the narrow road; the ground shook so severely that we were terrified.

It was one of the scariest things we had ever experienced. "The moving earthquake," as you might have guessed, was a semi-truck pulling a trailer with three humongous trees, logs actually. We watched as it went by. It was pretty cool actually, after it was over.

Well, we made it down the mountain road by the third afternoon. Vern was waiting for us as he said he would be. Of course, we didn't have cell phones back in 1982. Maybe this wasn't everyone's ideal honeymoon, but it was sweet for a couple of ex-hippies from California. We thoroughly enjoyed Lynne and Vern's hospitality for a few more days and then returned home chauffeured by Amtrak. This was the beginning of a love story that would challenge and test our commitment "through sickness and health, till death do us part" in a way we couldn't have imagined.

September 3, 2004

How could we have known that a routine visit to the chiropractor would change our lives forever? We saw Dr. Hancock in Prescott, Arizona, on a lovely sunny day. We always tried to enjoy the 75-mile trip from Williams. We entertained ourselves, looking for wildlife along the side of the roadway. There was always a possibility of seeing deer, and since between the Mountains of Williams and the mountains of Prescott, there are miles of plains, there's always a chance of seeing herds of pronghorn deer. Being a lover of birds of prey in the wild, this trip always allowed me to see quite a few hawks that had ample food on the plains. It was a long trip, but we made a day of it. We loved to go to Coco's restaurant for lunch. They had tortilla soup that Donna just loved. The other restaurant we frequented was a buffet. The Golden Dragon had great food. My only problem was going back for seconds and thirds. And we'd usually stop at Walmart there to pick up things we couldn't get in Williams. Being a small town, Williams didn't have all the big box stores those bigger cities had. Of course, that's the whole reason we chose Williams. With only a population of 4,000 people nestled in the mountains with forest all around, it was a perfect quaint town to retire in. I was 12 years from retirement, but when we received an inheritance from Donna's parents, we thought, "Why wait? Why not buy a house and enjoy this beautiful place, an hour from the Grand Canyon."

On this particular day, there was no indication that anything was wrong with my wife, Donna. Sometimes, the long trip gave her pain in her lower back, but after several car accidents over the years, it was expected. This was the whole reason we were going to the chiropractor in the first place. We originally started seeing Dr. Hancock in Tucson when we lived there. As it happened, just at the same time we moved, Dr. Hancock opened a part-time practice in Prescott. He would spend half the week in Prescott and half the week in Tucson. He was pretty clever, building a business in a new city before closing down the business in Tucson and moving to Prescott full-time, which was his goal. When we heard he was in Prescott, we gladly made the trip to see him.

We waited our turn in his busy office, which wasn't a chore considering how pleasant and friendly Dr. Hancock and his team were. Soon, Donna was lying down on the table for her adjustment. It wasn't long before Dr. Hancock noticed that Donna was beginning to turn white as he worked on her. This set off an alarm in Dr. Hancock's mind. This wasn't the first time this had happened on his table. One of his patients in the past had had a heart attack on his table, and he wasn't about to take any chances. Immediately, he jumped into action. As it turned out, St. Joseph's Hospital was right across the street from his office. There was no need to call an ambulance. We put Donna in our van and were there in minutes, quicker than an ambulance could have been there. From my first marriage, my son Ryan happened to be with us on this trip and helped me get Donna to the hospital as quickly as possible. Thank God, everything went smoothly like clockwork in this emergency. As it happened, the emergency room wasn't busy that day. The doctor on call was able to see us almost at once. As the doctor began his examination, Dr. Hancock showed up. That's the kind of person he was; he put all the other patients on hold and ran over to check on my wife. The emergency doctor ran tests on Donna, but they all returned negative. Blood tests, and CT scans, all were negative. That's when the doctor started asking Donna questions. These weren't hard questions, "What day is it?", "What month is it?" "Who is the president of the United States?", "What state are we in?" Donna couldn't answer any of the simple questions. This led to the doctor taking even more tests. He told us he could instantly authorize these tests as the emergency room doctor. He told us it wasn't like a regular doctor's office where you take a couple of tests and return two weeks later for results, then order more tests if necessary. But even still, the tests came back negative.

It was then that he gave us his unofficial diagnosis. He said he couldn't find anything physically wrong with Donna. Then, he dropped the bomb that changed our lives forever. His diagnosis was that she had some chronic mild dementia of an unknown etiology. It was September 3rd, 2004. A day full of unanswered questions, full of unknowns. A new beginning down a road that we couldn't possibly imagine. I don't remember much about that extremely long ride home that day. I know the doctor told us of tests that needed to be done on Donna's heart and that we needed to see a neurologist. Again, it was our good fortune to find Dr. Hoover in Flagstaff.

Flagstaff, Arizona, is about 35 miles from our house. It was not too far to see the specialist we needed for the next step in a journey that would last 14 years. In 2004, Alzheimer's was still a disease that scientists were still learning about. Research was relatively new, even then. Dr. Hoover prescribed two drugs, Namenda and Aricept. I didn't know how these worked, but I do know that for us, they were like miracle drugs. Donna had lost the ability to write or draw as she always had. For someone who did pencil portraits and calligraphy, this was devastating. But slowly, with time, the ability to write came back. Drawing was another matter. Her memory, in general, seemed to be restored for a time. After the first year, Donna asked to be taken off the Aricept. This Aricept medicine made her mind race, which was hard for a person with a one-track mind. Being an artist, you need to focus. On the other hand, I always had five things on my mind simultaneously. Donna's ability to recreate someone's likeness from a picture was amazing. It was like she traced it. She was talented at doing calligraphy as well. She used to pick out scripture in the Bible and write it on special paper; then, I would carve out the space in a piece of bark from the pines in Colorado. Then, she would cover the plaques in polyurethane and sell them on consignment in a craft store in Colorado Springs, where we lived at the time. Namenda was a medicine that Donna took for most of her sickness. In the last couple of years; the doctor took her off the medication because it wasn't affecting her condition.

Our minds were spinning, just thinking about what lay ahead of us. I couldn't imagine how I would pay the medical bills that were to come. I had no idea how I was going to take care of my wife and work at the same time. We didn't know anything about Alzheimer's. Donna was diagnosed with "early onset Alzheimer's". She was only 56 years old. That's not old, and this was supposed to be a disease of the "old." You know, people in their 70's and 80's. Our whole world was turned upside down. Our faith was tested beyond measure, but we knew our God would not fail us. "Yeah, though I walk through the valley of death, I will fear no evil, for thou art with me." Though our troubles were now many, God was there and blessed us through the whole experience.

Early-onset Alzheimer's is rare; only 5% of people in the U.S. with Alzheimer's get it. They can be as young as 30 or up to 65 years old. Donna was 56 years old. We don't know what caused it in her. As far as we can tell, no one in her family had it. There are some possibilities we can try and tie it to drug use when she was younger or when she banged her head hard against our brick bedroom wall in Tucson. But thankfully, those mostly aren't the reasons. The fact is, we probably will never know. They can do an autopsy on the brain after her death, which is the only way they can determine it is Alzheimer's Disease. They can check her DNA chromosomes 1, 14, 19, and 21, all of which have been discovered to have genes that could cause Alzheimer's. (The Forgetting Alzheimer's Portrait of an Epidemic by David Shenk, pg. 150).

The Day-to-Day Routine

One of the most necessary objectives when caring for an Alzheimer's patient is to try and give them a daily routine. It's just that it isn't always possible when you are the only caregiver who also works full-time. My company Safeway Grocers, and all the employees and managers at my store, bent over backward to help me through this anxious time. It was like the assistant manager said during my yearly review one year. It wasn't my best review, and she said, "You've got to admit you've had a rough year." My mental state wasn't good, and those who worked in the meat department with me suffered. I wish it had been different, but my mood changed, and I was often irritable. Nevertheless, help finally came for me through circumstances in a total stranger's life that brought us together.

God works in mysterious ways, and that's precisely what happened in October of 2010. Our friend, Sachiko, worked as a caregiver out of offices at the local Senior Center in Williams, where we lived.

One day, while she was there, a woman walked in looking for work. They didn't have a position open, but Sachiko told her she knew someone who was looking for help with his wife, who had Alzheimer's disease. At the time, I only needed someone to be a daytime companion for Donna and maybe do a little cleaning and cooking. I was willing to trade rent for help because I had no extra money for the service. It just happened that Annie needed a place to stay because she was going through a divorce and had moved away from her husband. Annie was a Godsend. We had a three-bedroom house, so Annie moved into the extra bedroom. Whenever I was off work, she was free to visit her friends. At night, Annie cooked for us; sometimes we ate together, sometimes not. But after dinner, Annie would always retreat to her room for privacy. She was a quiet, kind, sweet Christian woman. She stayed with us for over a year until she returned to the Philippines to care for her sick father.

While Annie was still living with us one night, she went out with Sachiko to church around five in the evening. It had usually been okay to leave Donna for an hour or so. Erin, our neighbor, said she would check in on Donna and give me a call at work to let me know how she was doing. It was around six when she called, and everything was fine. I got off the job at 7 p.m. and would be coming home immediately, so none of us were too worried. I say "none of us" because all our close neighbors and friends were concerned with Donna's safety and well-being. Next-door neighbors to our right, Lowell and Tina, would come by if I called and asked. Next to them were our close friends from church, Dave and Sharon, who would be there in 2 minutes if I called them. On our left side, Roger and Erin came by when I asked. They rented our old single-wide where we lived before; we had moved into our new manufactured home we had put on our second lot. We were initially the first house in our tract of homes and now the second home. Many neighbors knew of us because they drove by our houses daily, and many knew of my wife's condition. More than once, I would find out, after the fact, that a neighbor we hardly knew had brought Donna home when they had found her wandering down our neighborhood street. We lived in a tract of houses seven miles out of town, surrounded by country. You can imagine how comforting it was for me when I had no choice but to go to work, to know so many people cared and watched out for Donna.

I always called Donna when I got off from work to let her know I was on the way home. It was getting harder and harder for her to operate the phone. That night, when Annie was gone, she tried to answer the phone and couldn't get the phone to her ear correctly. She could hear me talking but couldn't respond to what I was saying. She looked forward to my calls all afternoon. The frustration was so incredible she just started screaming. I can still hear the screams. I was coming home as fast as I could without speeding. Out of the corner of my eye, I saw the elk coming out of the forest. At 7:30 p.m., darkness had already covered the night sky. I had barely enough time to grab the steering wheel in my truck when I hit this elk running full speed across the road in front of me. BAM! I hit him square across the front of the truck. We both stopped instantly. The whole front of my truck was caved in. The elk was lying helpless on the ground. I called nine-one-one, and they were sending someone. I was only a block from the Department of Public Safety substation. Then, I called my neighbors, Dave and Sharon, and asked them to check on her. I had left her screaming on the phone. It was snowing that night, and when Dave got to my house, Donna was outside with no coat on. Dave returned her to the house and stayed with her until I got home. I don't know how, but somehow, the phone turned on, and the "leave a message recording" recorded Donna's blood-curdling screams. I still have that tape recording from the phone today.

This is why caregivers need a network of support. This is how a crazy lifestyle situation can be overcome and lived through by having a support network. Many aspects of being your spouse's caregiver don't even enter your mind when your journey begins. Donna had false teeth our whole marriage. Unlike my mother, who had dentures, she never took them out at night. I never saw her with her teeth out in all our years of marriage until 2006. It wasn't until she had to have a hip replacement. Because, at the time, it was a major surgery, she had to take off her wedding ring and take out her teeth. For the first time in twenty-four years, Donna was utterly transformed into a woman twenty years older than she was. I was shocked. I had no idea there would be a change so drastic. This instantly became one of my first tests in growth toward becoming a loving person and caregiver. I had to make an immediate decision, one that would be like hundreds of instant choices you make as a new caregiver of a loved one. Do I react from the mind or the heart? Will I be repulsed by this or instantly (almost) accept it? What choice did I have? I loved her. I chose to accept this temporary condition. My compassion for her was increasing as our trials were growing.

The surgery was a success, and after Donna recovered from the immediate effects of the surgery, she put her teeth back in the next day or so. Never did I bring up to her how she looked, how her appearance had changed. No doubt she was humbled by the experience, as was I. Little did I realize that in a few short years, I would be the one doing her daily routine of taking out her dentures and then putting the denture cream on them that aligned them so they would fit properly in her mouth—something I had never seen her do. This wasn't a game or interesting new experience to try. Donna's teeth needed to be aligned correctly, or not only would she be in pain, but it would be difficult for her to eat. The last thing she needed was to lose weight. She had enough stress in her life without being unable to chew her food correctly and without pain.

You see when we first began this journey of Alzheimer's, I had no idea how often things would happen that I had no control over, and neither did Donna. And, just like that unexpected facial change I had just witnessed, there would be many changes to her personality that I wouldn't see coming until it happened. I had no clue how often Donna would do something or say something she had no control over. Her reaction to things and conversations was slowly being warped by a disease that was not her fault. She was becoming Doctor Jekyll and Mrs. Hyde right before my eyes. My emotions are like any person's. When I said I had to make the decision instantly to not overreact to her behavior, I didn't mean to give you the impression that I was always successful. No, not at first. This is the 'Journey of Love' that I was beginning. The love that would grow and mature took years. It took going through all that we went through to become the person I needed to be to survive the ravages of Alzheimer's.

Probably one of the hardest things to accept is that I was 'everything' to her, not just emotionally, but literally. She'd gotten to the point where she couldn't speak, and I was becoming her total caregiver/parent/nurse. And there was no way at the time I believed I was ready or competent to fulfill that position. I truly believe unless you've been a caregiver or a counselor to caregivers, you can't understand that everything in your life is going insane while you're watching your spouse die. You're trying to learn to cook, pay the bills, and figure out what she's trying to say. I've cooked some in my life, but I wouldn't say I like cooking like 'cooks' like cooking. My spice is ketchup and lots of butter and sour cream on the microwaved baked potato. But now, my life was planning meals, portion control, and ensuring the food was cooked right. I had to ensure she could chew the food with her dentures and wouldn't choke on the food.

I had to handle all these new ways of living. Cooking healthy was now my responsibility. It was always Donna's job to motivate me to eat healthily. When we lived in Tucson, we'd get these discount coupons from the Sunday paper for the Sweet Tomato Restaurant. We'd go after church on Sunday. It was an all-salad buffet, and I thought I'd walk away hungry. "What, no meat? At a buffet? I'm going to die."!!!! I lived. The more we went there, the more I liked it. I even learned some things like that fresh leafy stuff they called spinach was nothing like that slimy cooked stuff people have been trying to get me to eat my whole life. Each time we ate there, I'd try new vegetables. I learned to eat cauliflower and broccoli that I didn't like cooked. Okay, but I did have to draw the line at one point. Did you know people actually eat Brussels sprouts? Cooked or not, not me. I even heard they're healthy.

I took over the bills once, for about two or three months. I messed them up so quickly I gave them back to her to straighten out. My male ego was quenched, but I never touched them again until I had no choice. No more giving them back again, ever. I have trouble keeping track of everything. I wouldn't say I like paperwork very much. Now, I had to figure out the bank accounts, insurance policies, and keeping up with our monthly obligations. It wasn't foreign to me; even still, I realized how hard it must have been for the wives whose husbands took care of all the finances and then passed away, leaving them to figure everything out. We, husbands, are foolish not to appreciate how important and valuable our wives are for all they contribute to a marriage.

It hadn't been since I was single in my 20s that I did all my laundry, house cleaning, and grocery shopping. At first, when I started taking over these jobs, one by one, I was still working full-time. I would fix my wife's breakfast before I went to work and come home on my lunch hour to fix her lunch. After work, I would rush home and fix her dinner. Suddenly, you get a whole new outlook on what her real contribution was to this marriage partnership.

"I miss my best friend", I wrote in my journal on 12-27-2010. In a sense, I can't share my fears or worries with Donna anymore. Instead of comforting me like she used to, she still does, but then she internalizes my fear and starts worrying about whatever I might talk about, like money or work. For 29 years, she has been the one I turn to when I'm stressed out or need to talk about work. I have friends I can talk to about things, but no one can replace her being there with a compassionate shoulder to lean on after a rough day at work. I'm not like other guys who say they leave employment at work and never talk about it at home. You spend 40-plus hours with the people you work with, and you're not supposed to discuss it. Those guys are the same guys who aren't concerned with their wives 'day.' It's communication that makes and saves a marriage. Well, now, I can't talk about these things. She gets all upset for me. Her emotions are amplified, and she doesn't need the extra stress. Just getting through each day is more than enough for her to deal with.

I realize now how much I depended on her; I can do nothing to replace that. Our conversations are almost nothing as I write this. I can talk to her, and she can respond with yes or no answers, but she forgets the second half of the sentence before she finishes the first half. My frustration goes to my heart, watching her try so hard to remember the word that's inching to the tip of her tongue but dissolving as it almost comes out. I used to be able to help finish sentences for her, but now she starts talking so much of the time, and she's in her own little world. Then I'm lost trying to decipher what prompted her thinking process. You must understand that this person used to beat me at Scrabble every time we played. It would have required 'prayer and fasting' for me to beat her. And, the one or two times I did beat her, I felt like calling all my family and friends for a celebration party. Words are essential to a writer; she not only used to do crossword puzzles, but she also made up her own. She wrote Christian papers on depression and encouragement.

Donna loved to write poetry. The church we went to even printed a book of poems she had written. Imagine having a skill with using words, and now she can't even complete a sentence on her own.

Donna had always loved writing. As a child, she would write letters to famous actors, once even to President Eisenhower. And now, she can't even grasp a pen without help, let alone write with it. Words the average person throws around like they were pennies not worth the time to step down and pick up. Words like having a million dollars in your savings account and slowly, not all at once, watching it dwindle away with no power to stop it until it's gone, never to return. All the while, I was standing on the sideline watching the game being lost, longing to go in and play to help her score a touchdown, but there were no more touchdowns in this game. This game is over long before the last quarter is even played. There will be no victory in sight for this game. In her book 'Learning to Speak Alzheimer's,' Joanne Koenig Coste says, 'Remember that the emotions behind failing words are far more important than the words themselves – and the emotions need to be watched. Although many losses occur with this disease, assume that the patient can still register feelings that matter.'

Just today, when we were going to Flagstaff, Donna said, "What are you and those people...". I said, "What people, Pete and Ellie, people from church, Leo and Dorothy?" She interrupted, "No, no. I don't want to do that." She meant, "I'm not in the mood to play the guessing game you always play; don't even go there." She knew my usual routine at going through a list of people we knew, and by the time I'd rattled off six or seven names, she'd forgotten whatever she wanted to say. She was tired, and it wasn't worth it "just drop it." When I used to try and finish her sentence, I wasn't always helping, and I would frustrate Donna. It would be best if you watched what the person was feeling. Is it worth trying and pursuing an answer, or is it better to drop it? Sometimes, you can only reach over with your loving arms, hug her, and acknowledge her frustration.

There's a lot of swallowing your pride when you're a caregiver. Humility is one of the first acts of love that must be learned. It can no longer be what "I" want all the time. I was selfish and self-centered during the first half of our marriage. Those days were gone. A scripture says, "Love is patient, love is kind. It does not envy; it does not boast; it is not proud; it is not rude; it is not self-seeking; it is not easily angered; it keeps no record of wrong; love does not delight in evil but rejoices with the truth. It always protects, always trusts, always hopes, always perseveres. Love never fails. (1 Corinthians 13:4-8 NIV) Being a caregiver, I had to learn all these aspects of love. It wasn't easy, and I wasn't always successful initially. But I loved Donna. I felt the whole time she loved me, even when I was blind to her needs. She stood by me when I failed her. There was no way on God's earth I would abandon her when she needed me most. She was the one who taught me God's love, and now was the time for me to return the favor.

CHAPTER 2

The Unravelling of the Mind

Learning patience takes going through the first and second stages (mild, moderate). And you think, ah, now I've got it. But the truth is your patience hasn't even been tested yet. It's like my training in the military for war. My Army drill sergeant used to tell us, "Nothing you learn here will matter when you get to Nam!". Trainings, nothing compared to the real thing. The late stage or severe stage is a whole new ballgame. I can see already we're just beginning an experience that all the reading in the world will not prepare me. I'd read several books about peopled experiences, like "The Long Goodbye" by President Ronald Reagan's daughter and what their family went through. Dancing with Dementia by Christine Breyden was about her life as an Alzheimer's patient. It helped so much with my perspective of Donna and her worth. Miss Bryden described the loss of respect from others just because she was declining yet still could think and speak of her life. Yet, even though each book gave me good advice and information, nothing prepared me for my madness as a caregiver. As in the four months of training in the Army, most men got before being shipped to Nam nothing prepared them for living through the insanity of war. Ultimately, I never went to Vietnam, but I had my battle here at home.

One morning, I had coffee with our Pastor, Andy. We were talking about Donna's communication problems. She wants to say something but not being able to get it out. He said it was the same with his twin 2-year-old girls. They could talk enough to be able to say what they want. And when they can't get it out, they get frustrated, as do he and his wife, Melissa. It's the same for

Donna and me; the frustration causes anger. My talk with Andy reminded me that Donna was becoming my child.

Everything had changed by that time. The level of care required has gone to a new level. I was showering her one morning, and as is our usual routine, when it came time for me to wash Donna's feet, she had her back to the shower door leaning against the shower wall; she usually put her arm against the wall for support. When she did that this time, she slipped on the water with her right foot when I lifted her left foot to be cleaned. She fell against the door and out onto the floor. Her legs caught the bottom of the shower right at the buttocks, where there was a metal lip. She slid the rest of the way to the floor along that metal line, creating two giant bruises on the back of her legs. She was more scared than hurt. I could break her fall a little so she didn't hit her head, but it scared both of us. She halfway cried out of fear, but not for long. The worst part was how the bruises looked the next day. Each leg had a bruise at least 2" deep and 5" wide. They were black and blue. It wasn't enjoyable and wasn't very pleasant. It was the first injury Donna received under my care. It didn't bother her much, and she didn't complain about it except a couple of times she sat down. I felt so bad I wanted to crawl into a hole and die. It's like seeing your child get hurt right before your eyes because you weren't careful enough, and now she is suffering because of you. I couldn't take it back. I couldn't kiss it and make it better. I'm her caregiver. How could I have let this happen? Telling yourself "Nobody is perfect" doesn't help at that moment. It's hard enough for her without me adding more suffering to her situation. And, of course, it's hard enough for me mentally without causing myself one more thing to beat myself up over.

We went to Bookman's used bookstore today. I had Donna stand behind me while I looked at the audiobooks. I bent down to look at the lower shelves, and she lost sight of me. Suddenly, I could hear her ask herself, "Where is he?" with fear. It only took a minute or so for this to happen. She became terrified that she was alone and that I had left her. I jumped up and let her know I was right there. I comforted her, and she said she was alright later in the car. She realized it scared me and told me she was okay now. There is no time, no moment when I can take any situation for granted. Caregivers know what I'm talking about. Again, it's like taking care of a child. You cannot expect them to make mature decisions or understand the anger of life. You cannot expect them to know your thoughts or assume they understand what's going on. The stress grows as the disease progresses. I saw a TV documentary where, in one case, a woman had to quit work to take care of her mother. One day, while walking, the mother kept picking pebbles and putting them in her mouth. Then, when asked to give them to her daughter, she refused. The daughter had to dig them out of her mother's mouth like you would a child, resisting every minute. The constant effort of dealing with her mom just...made her stop and cry.

One night, Donna was looking for her shoes. I found them in the bathroom and took them to the bedroom. Then she got up again to see the shoes and wouldn't believe they were her shoes. I said you wear these shoes every day. She said, "No, they're not my shoes." Once I put them on her, she realized they were indeed her shoes. She wears them all day and naps in them, so she felt them missing from her feet when she went to bed. After putting them on and realizing they were hers, she didn't need them on for sleeping. Again, the next night, I could tell Donna was thinking about her shoes, so I showed them to her before I took them off for bed. She looked at them like those aren't my shoes! But I reminded her about last night's episode, so she took my word for it. Going to the bathroom later, I looked, and she was lying on the bed with her shoes on. I couldn't help but laugh.

Immediately after her diagnosis, Donna quit driving. I tried to get her to drive again, but she refused. Her selfless response was "What do you want me to kill somebody?" The truth is she was still capable of driving. It had only been a few days since she was diagnosed. In the same way, some family and friends dismissed her from conversations as if she was in the last stage already. She could still think and talk and understand things. She was just slower reacting than before. I could see when we visited people how they would ignore her as if she'd already lost her mind. This upset me, but Donna always made excuses for them. That's the kind of person she was. That very thing showed that Donna was still Donna. It is written, "Love does not keep a record of wrongs." That was indeed the kind of love that she had. She always showed me the character of Christ through her actions, always forgiving, always looking at the best side, always persevering. It would be a few more years before I had that kind of love.

Again, in her book "Dancing with Dementia," Christine Breyden writes *"The Myths and Fears about Dementia," the stereotype of someone in the later stages of the disease that causes dementia – gives rise to the stigma that isolates us. You say we do not remember, so we cannot understand. We do not know, so it's okay to distance yourself from us. And you treat us with fear and dread. We cannot work, we cannot drive, we cannot contribute to society. I am overseen for signs of odd words or behavior. My opinion is no longer sought, and I am thought to lack insight, so it does not matter that I am excluded. But if I have understanding and can speak clearly or write about my experiences, then I am said to lack credibility as a true representative of people with dementia; why is this so? Maybe it is because the stereotype and the stigma are based on the end stages of dementia. But dementia is not just an end state; it is a journey from diagnosis to death, with many steps along the way. My battle for credibility in making this journey was, at first, lonely."* Mrs. Breyden knew firsthand as a person with Alzheimer's what it felt like to be dismissed as a person. What a gift it was for me to read this book. It opened my eyes even more to see my beautiful wife as a person who's alive and deserves respect. Right up to the end of her life, you could see Donna's personality in her behavior. She was always there, so you can imagine how frustrating it was for her to be treated like a child along the way. How horrible it must have been for her to lose the ability to put a simple sentence together. To know what you want to say, to see people staring at you, waiting for you to get the words out, and you just can't; your intellect is still there; you're not an idiot; it's right on the tip of your tongue. Then it's gone. And she knows she's better than that. But she also knows she's slipping away. I was reading to Donna from this same book describing what it was like for Christine, and Donna exclaimed, "That's like me; that's what I feel like." It comforted her that someone else was going through the same thing, and she understood. This comment was made in her 7th year of Alzheimer's. She spoke with clarity and knew what she was saying. My point is she was still herself, not all there, but not all gone,

One night, Donna asked if she should go to a home because she knew she was getting worse. I said no, I need you here with me. It just so happens I was reading in the book "At the Heart of Alzheimer's" by Carol Simpson, the chapter on putting your loved one in a home for their benefit and yours. They talked about how hard it is to have feelings of guilt, shame, or worry. I said to myself, like they quoted someone might say, I can't do that! But they pointed out that when the time comes, it's a better life for the person who has Alzheimer's and for the caregiver. How could I betray my best friend that way? How could I not do it if I loved her so much? Three times, I put my wife in an Assisted Living House. The first time, she lasted three weeks. There's a home in Flagstaff called Rose Arbor. I had taken four days off work and stayed with her for those four days. But on the fifth day, I had to go back to work. Everything seemed fine. We watched TV and walked together, and I slept on the couch downstairs. The home manager, Becky, allowed me to stay even though that didn't usually happen. On the fifth day, when I got ready to leave, Donna had a horrible realization. She realized I was going to leave her, and she had to stay home. She got so upset. She said, "I can't believe he's leaving me here, and I can't believe he would do this to me!" I had to go to work; I couldn't stay. You talk about feeling guilty. All the way to work and through my whole shift, it took all of my energy to do my job and not break down crying. Donna would wake up at two in the morning and start screaming. This went on for three weeks. Finally, Becky had to ask me to come and get Donna and take her home. She was disturbing the other patients too severely. They were having too much trouble sleeping, disrupting the patient's routine. It wouldn't be long before new circumstances dictated making another try at placing her in another home.

I brought Donna home, and things returned to our everyday insane life. Nighttime dramas were increasing. I got mad one night because, at 12.30 AM, she wanted to shower and wash her hair to eliminate the itching on her scalp. I was angry, but she wouldn't take no for an answer. I was tired and needed a break, but I did it. Arguing with someone who is not thinking straight in the first place doesn't accomplish anything. She woke up the following day not remembering what happened but remembering I was mad at her. She asked me first thing, "Did I do something wrong?" I explained what happened the night before and apologized for getting angry. She's a child now, and I have to get over the inconveniences of this disease that I have to deal with. This is where a more profound love is learned. Sure, I loved her when everything was fine, but will I love her through the sickness, especially an illness of the mind?

In June 2013, the doctor and I got Donna a wheelchair. She was walking slowly, and we thought it would help her save her strength. After she received the chair and started sitting in it, she walked twice across the room to the bathroom and then never walked again. I had no experience with someone wheelchair-bound. The first night I transferred Donna to the bed, she was completely dead weight. She didn't know how to help me, so I tried to pick her up with my arms instead of my legs. I picked her up, twisted from the waist, and almost threw her onto the bed. That's when I felt the pain of my groin tearing. It was excruciating. I didn't even know what a hernia was, but I was about to find out. I was still working as a meat cutter at the Safeway store of Williams. I couldn't get off work to get operated on because the holidays were coming up, and we were short of help. That was the final straw at that time. I had to put Donna in a home for the second time. The Ponderosa House was within the city of Williams. I was able to visit her usually twice a day. I was very protective of her and checked on her regularly. This was a welcomed relief, to be honest. I was working my 8-hour shifts with a hernia, and the constant pain made me irritable. I'm sure my fellow employees would agree. I learned to slide the 50 lb boxes of meat onto my cart instead of picking them up. I walked a lot slower, too. It wasn't until Dec 6 of that year, after Thanksgiving, that I got my hernia operation. But here again, I have to be grateful. I went through a lot of pain, but I've never had a problem with the mesh in my abdomen since the operation.

It was when Donna went into the home that I could travel again. Half my siblings were in southern California and my grandkids were in Tucson, AZ. I've always loved driving on long trips. LA is close to 500 miles from Williams. I would drive across the desert at night when I went out to see my brothers and sister. I took my time and always stopped in Kingman to eat before crossing the desert. It was a great time for me to unwind and always a happy time with my family. I generally stayed for two days. I'd arrive Saturday morning in Anaheim around 6 a.m. Then, after visiting, I would leave Sunday around 2 p.m. or 3 p.m. to come home. Each night when I was away, I'd call Donna at the home at 6 p.m. and talk to her. Linda or Junior, the husband-and-wife caregivers, would answer and give the phone to Donna. We didn't speak for long. It was mostly for her to hear my voice. I didn't like being away from Donna, yet I knew I had to take advantage of the situation and get away. And besides, Junior and Linda took good care of Donna. Donna was in this home for about a year when I retired in 2014. It was then that my financial circumstances started to change. I went to the Social Security office to see if we could get the $94, a paper from them said she was due every month. She hadn't worked much over the years, so she didn't pay in much. As it turned out, the lady at the Social Security office said Donna didn't qualify for any money. She said that the paper that estimated her benefits was wrong. This wasn't very pleasant, but the lady pointed out that if I wanted to retire early, I could retire when I turned 62 in three months. I thought about it quickly. If I waited until I turned 65, I could get an extra $500 monthly. I just figured if I needed $500, I'd get a part-time job somewhere. So, I decided to retire when I turned 62. It would take three months for the process to be complete right after my birthday. Wow, I thought I'd always work, and before going to social security that day, retirement wasn't something I thought I'd ever do. But now, this is where the twist comes in. This is where God's and my plan were a whole different story. The lady told me besides two small retirements from Safeway and Albertson's; I had a vested retirement from my years in the union in California. The union had locked in my time back in 1994. I didn't know anything about it. I was going to get almost $500 a month for that time. Man, I was ecstatic, but God wasn't through yet. It turns out since Donna was my spouse, and I had paid so much to S.S. over my working career that she was qualified to receive $ 1,000 a month. Amazing, simply amazing. I went to the office that day looking for an extra $94 a month. I left that office that day three months from retirement with at least $500 more than I expected per month. The $1000 that Donna received I was then able to use for my copay at the nursing home of $892 a month. And the remaining $108 was mine to spend on any toiletries or over-the-counter meds she might use or clothes she might need. Just as my life had changed when Donna entered the home a year before, now it would undergo another significant change. Retirement at 62, unbelievable, retirement at 62!

Although my expenses and savings went down at this time, it was a far different story back in the summer of 2011. We applied for government assistance and were turned down. As it turned out, I made too much money to be 'rated poor.' So, in the late summer or early fall of that year, I took a family leave of absence without pay to become poor enough to qualify by the end of the year. We knew God would provide a way, and He did too! It was not a simple decision or an overnight whim. Lives were at stake, and I remember telling my boss the story in the bible of the woman who had begun preparing her last meal to sit down with her son to eat and then die. Starvation, I did not see that in the future of my wife and me. And yet, when I chose to stay home and care for Donna because we had no caregivers and knew we would have no income, I remembered the story. I also remembered how God provided for the woman and her son when Elijah asked her to share her last meal. It all comes down to the faith and belief we will be provided for. There wasn't just one miracle either; miracles were coming out of the woodwork in the form of family and friends. Donations of time, money, food, and prayer came from all over the country. Quietly, my brother Curtis and his wife Sherry, my former boss Gary and his wife Pat in Texas, family members in California, and my brother Chuck and his wife Pam in Canada all sent money. Our friends Joe and Leslie in Colorado also supported us regularly. Leslie had been Donna's best friend. I think since we had all met in 1982. Friends like these are there for you in your time of need. Our friends and neighbors, Dave and Sharon, were there for us in many ways. What meant the most to me was the time they gave us; their visits were often. And for someone like me whose personality says, "I need someone to talk to", I truly appreciated those morning or evening visits.

Many friends from our church also gave, not to mention the donations from my fellow Safeway employees. Other neighbors came forward with offers of help if we needed it. I could hardly believe the generosity of so many wonderful people. One couple who were neighbors, we weren't necessarily that close, stopped me in the parking lot of the Safeway where I had worked. They said they had read our letter in the local newspaper. We sent a letter to the editorial page, asking them to help us to thank everyone who helped us. "Is there anything we can do? "Can you guys use some wood"? Our house at the time was only heated by wood because I couldn't afford to replace the propane furnace that was so old it wouldn't stay on anymore. I told them thanks and would let them know. When I saw them in the store three days later, I confessed I could use the wood but didn't want to ask (pride again). Evelyn, Tom's wife, said, 'You didn't ask; we asked you.' Admittedly, I was very relieved. By then, I had been out of work for five months and was pretty broke. Just moments before we ran into Tom and Evelyn, I had cashed in the spare change I had saved in a jar, like most older people. I got back 80 dollars. My checking account was empty, and my savings were down to 38 dollars. Knowing how many people cared for us was humbling but also very overwhelming. We hadn't paid any bills in 3 months but didn't go hungry. Our church family gave us money to pay for our electricity for six months; many others brought food. I couldn't have any other attitude except gratitude amid our trials when we had such an outpouring of love from so many people. Of course, Donna didn't grasp what was going on. She didn't even realize that I was supposed to be at work or think it was unusual that I was home every day. I could never discuss finances with her; when I explained things enough for her to understand, it would depress her, or she would turn to me and say 'thank you.'

With Alzheimer's patients, it's a mistake to think that their whole mental capacity is gone because they've become kids in many areas. Often, Donna would grasp for a moment the sacrifices I was making and thank me or look at me with her soft smile and say, "I love you." Our next-door neighbors Lowell and Tina were also always there if we needed them. When I finally got help through ALTCCS (Arizona Long Term Care), I felt guilty because I wanted to return to work to get a break from caregiving. A mental break. I soon had caregivers to help, and my job back at Safeway.

It was Thanksgiving 2013, around 7:30 p.m. when the fire happened. I was living alone. Donna had been in the home for a few months by then. It's just me and the three cats preparing to watch TV, after work. The lights were out in the living room when I filled the woodburning stove as full of wood as possible. I didn't want to mess with it the rest of the night. Theoretically, it was a good plan. I was leaving the kitchen when I noticed a red glow in the ceiling above the stove. The fire had gotten so hot it went up the chimney pipes and caught the ceiling on fire. It just so happened I had half a bucket of water on the kitchen floor. Everywhere I've lived since the 80's, I've had to conserve water. First, it was in the mountains of Colorado. Then, when we lived in Tucson, Arizona, for eight years. When we moved to Williams, we had to have our water delivered to our house, which could be expensive. So, whenever I turned the hot water tap on in the kitchen sink, I would catch the cold water in the bucket until it started to get warm to do the dishes. I grabbed the bucket of water and ran into the living room. I threw the water up to the ceiling. Then, I ran to the kitchen to refill the bucket. After I threw that water on the pipes, I called my friend Jimmy for help. It so happened he temporarily lived in his travel trailer in my backyard. Jimmy was a welder, and when I asked him if he had a fire extinguisher, what fortunate timing for me. He had recently received a box of 12 canisters of a new fire extinguisher. He still had eleven cans left. While Jimmy was grabbing his stuff, I put a chair on my living room table and then another chair on top of that. I climbed up the chairs and started punching holes in the ceiling. When Jimmy arrived, I had hit a big enough gap to stick my body into the rafters. That's when Jimmy handed me a can to spray the fire. Older single-wide trailers were known for going up in flames in minutes. That probably would have been the case here, except my single wide trailer had a metal roof. It was a 1973 model and only had 2 x 4 trusses. The whole top inside was covered with fiberglass insulation. The fire in the rafters was easy to spray out because they didn't have enough materials to burn. Soon, we had the fire out. The smoke damage was throughout the house, and some insulation and trusses were burned beyond repair. As it turned out, I never called the fire department. At 9 o'clock on Thanksgiving Eve, I called my Farm Bureau local agent, Don Dent. He was in his office by 8:00 a.m. the next day, Thanksgiving Day. He called and told me the calls had been made, and my claim was reported. None of this "it's a holiday, and you'll have to wait till Friday to get started." And where else but a small town would your insurance agent and his wife call you back and invite you to Thanksgiving dinner at their house? Don had been our insurance agent for years and knew my wife and that she was in a home. This is the advantage of living in a small town.

But the story doesn't end there. At the time of the fire, my other house, the manufactured home we had put on our second acre in 2006, was close to foreclosure. I was behind on my payments, and we had no renter in the house to help. When I was talking to the adjustor from Farm Bureau and Don Dent, he told me the single wide would be condemned, and I had a choice. They would either replace the single-wide with a comparable newer model that was up to code, or they could pay me off in cash. I explained to them that I would take the money to save my 7-year-old manufactured home if I had a choice. They were not only okay with that, but before they even had a total estimate of the damage and replacement cost, they cut me a check for $ 5,000 to save my manufactured home. This is customer service that is above and beyond. I committed to staying with Farm Bureau Williams as long as I lived in this town. Another example of how God turned a bad situation into a blessing.

Speaking of the benefits of a small town, I would like to relate a story that happened to us one day. I had picked my wife up from the home and stopped at Safeway before taking her home after our daily drive. Williams' main streets are one-way roads. I was parked across the street from

Safeway on Route 66 when I got Donna out of the car and into her wheelchair. Then, the chief of police, Herman Nixon, came up behind us. The Chief who saw what I was doing, diagonally turned his truck across the one-lane road, and stopped all traffic until I had my wife in her chair and pushed across to the Safeway parking lot. This was a clear example of "protect and serve" that a small-town chief of police gave to his town folk.

Everything in my life wasn't just trials. I had no idea what I was getting into back in 2010 when my friend Doc invited me to the Toastmasters meeting in Flagstaff. Well, I knew it was about improving your ability to speak in public, and that is precisely what I wanted to do. But Donna and I had never been to a meeting and had no idea how structured it was. The second reason I wanted to get involved with Toastmasters was because of 'networking.' If I was going to be a professional motivational speaker in my new career, networking was essential. Well, I was a little ahead of myself. My new job, while still working as a meat cutter, was as a caregiver, and I, indeed, wasn't professional at it. Nevertheless, I started going to Toastmasters meetings once a week. It wasn't long before an opportunity presented to me to provide an hour-and-a-half presentation about Alzheimer's to a Wisdom Seekers Club group. It was held at the Coconino County Human Resources Building. I was nervous, but our caregiver, Annie, created a PowerPoint for me. My friend Dave Martinez loaned me a video camera, and Doc videoed the whole talk. It was so fulfilling for me because it went well. As it turned out, I ran out of time, which was good because I was afraid I couldn't stretch it out that long. But Annie put all the material I had given her on slides, which helped tremendously. I also had a table where I displayed all the books on Alzheimer's I had read. I was so happy when it was over, but glad I did it. Doing that long talk this early in my speaking journey took away the fear of whether I could do it. Plus, now, with the film, I could analyze where my weak points were and what I could improve on, like eye contact with the audience or voice fluctuation and gestures to emphasize my points. This then led to other opportunities. I talked with my friend John Moore, the Mayor of Williams, who opened the door for me to speak at the Rotary Club meeting in town. I thought you could only talk to the group about community service issues. But John felt this subject would be educational and valuable to the community business leaders in the club. After this, I also gave a talk at the Lions Club of Williams. I began to see if I became an 'expert' in Alzheimer's, opportunities could present themselves for me to give other talks. There was a downside to this that hit me one night. The problem was the more I studied Alzheimer's, the more I saw my future with Donna. Who wants to be an expert in a subject that rips out your heart when you're going through it? A double-edged sword, I guess.

One night, I gave a talk at a Toastmasters meeting called 'Can there be humor with Alzheimer's?'. That night, Donna came with me to the forum. Donna was seven years into the illness at the time. I received good reviews from the group, but the biggest compliment came from my friend, the elder of our group, Ray. Ray said, making Donna smile and even laugh was the highlight of the speech. Toastmasters was an outlet for me, but when I could, I brought Donna, and she shared my accomplishments. She never lost her sense of humor. Over the years, I've stayed in Toastmasters. Sometimes, things got rough at home, and I dropped out for a while. Usually, these turbulent times were when I slipped back into my depression. Always though I got tired of being down, I would get back into Toastmasters. I love public speaking, especially when I'm teaching. I had other speaking experiences. I used to represent our church, filling in at the rescue mission in Flagstaff. Once a month, I preached to homeless men, hoping to encourage them not to give up. This eventually led to the opportunity to do substitute preaching in a couple of churches in town that needed someone to fill in when the pastors couldn't be there. I had another hobby that helped me get through each week. My friend Ed and I would go to karaoke at the Canyon Club bar in town. I love to sing, and we would go and have one drink that I sipped on for 2 hours. Usually, we sang 2 or 3 songs before the crowd shuffled in around 10 p.m. when we would leave. Another place I got to sing was in church. I've been blessed with the opportunity to sing solos on some Sunday mornings. I could no longer be committed to singing in the church choir, but I could learn a song to sing in the church for a service. I love singing about God's love and mercy.

I also had other goals and projects that kept me going. I had piles of 'treasures' lying around my yard that I was going to do something with someday. I had crafts I was going to do and had collected hubcaps off the freeway medians that I would polish and sell. I even knew how to make bird feeders out of hubcaps. Another idea was how to make clocks out of hubcaps. The truth is I started writing this book in 2010. But none of these projects were completed while I cared for Donna. They gave me hope for what I might still accomplish someday, but I had no time or genuine desire to work on extra stuff. I barely had the mental and physical energy to make it through every day. Eventually, I had to accept that I needed to get rid of many of my treasures in the yard, which added more stress every time I looked out the back window. It's just more work cluttering up my yard and mind.

In all that was going on in my life, it finally occurred to me one day that this wasn't about who the person with Alzheimer's was becoming but who I was becoming. I felt I had to find a purpose beyond my life as a caregiver. You might say, 'What do you mean, who am I becoming?' This is a fair question, but one that a caregiver must answer. Again, you might say, 'You don't have time to worry about the future; you're too busy with the present.' I understand because even to write in my journal, I had to sacrifice sleep. I waited until after Donna was finally asleep to write down the day's activities and my thoughts about what was happening. What was that question again? Oh yeah, who was I becoming? I notice how impatient I am with little things and how much impatience is because I'm inconvenienced. I also noticed that after I decided to use my experiences to help others, I started paying more attention to the details of this experience. As I was journaling, I not only wrote down funny or daily occurrences that happened, but I also wrote down the things that made me angry. As therapists will tell you, writing things down is like confession; it gets it out and off your chest. One of these frustrating, irritating really makes me mad things I wrote about in Chapter 3 is her constantly getting back up after she's gone to bed at night. But then it hit me one day. I can't go on like this anymore. Where is the love I'm supposed to be learning? Where is the 'love is patient, love is kind' behavior? I had to rebuke myself. One night, I gave a speech at Toastmasters titled "You can feel sorry for yourself or fulfill yourself". I had spent enough time feeling sorry for myself, thinking about Donna dying. I finally told myself Donna's not dead; she's alive. If I love her and I've grown in that love, I need to show it. I need to wake up. Otherwise, we both will die.

The day-to-day struggle as a caregiver wears on a person, but for the patient, that struggle only lasts as long as they remember it. I remember going to the doctor once with Donna for a shoulder problem with which she had a lot of pain. He said the one good thing about Alzheimer's is she will forget the pain. At first, when he said it, I thought that's kind of cold. But later, when she experienced pain from different medical problems and forgot the next day, I realized what a blessing it was and that the doctor was right. Now I could see the forgetting as a gift. It wasn't just medical pain she'd forget. If we had argued, she would have forgotten about it later. If she hears about a tragedy on the news, she gets upset but forgets about it quickly. So, even though forgetting is the main problem with Alzheimer's, it was a tremendous benefit at times. My friend Ed called it the serenity of forgetting.

It's heartbreaking to see an intelligent person lose their memory. When it's your loved one, you want to do something for them, but mostly, all you can do is watch. One day, Donna looked in the bathroom mirror and didn't know who she was looking at. She called me into the bathroom to help her. When I arrived, she pointed to the mirror and said, "Who is that?". It kind of shocks you at first. "It's you; who do you think it is?" I didn't say that out loud; it's just your first reaction. I gently told her it was her. This was one of those 'heartbreaking' times. It kills me to see the fear forgetting causes her. When you look at her face and see the confusion. Confusion leads to anxiety. Ordinary people can adjust their thinking. They can search for an answer to the confusion or ask someone to help, in the situation. How do you ask for help when 10 minutes after the confusion you've forgotten what confused you? You've forgotten what? You're you? All that remains is fear. You can't read the person's mind as a caregiver. If you're lucky, you were there to see what happened and can address the issue as soon as possible.

It got to the point when Donna could only be left alone for five minutes at a time, and that's only when she was occupied with eating or watching her favorite preacher, Joyce Meyers, on the television. She can sit alone for short periods when she is in a good mood and has nothing on her mind. That's when I could maybe do dishes, start the laundry, or begin fixing a meal. But one day, I broke the rules. A caregiver came over for a few hours to give me a respite. Carol wasn't one of our regular caregivers; she was our neighbor from a few blocks away. But she was a self-employed caregiver, so she knew what she was doing and offered to help when I needed a short break. When she was leaving, I walked her out to her car. My wife was eating her soup at the kitchen table, when we went outside. I had forgotten to tell Donna I was going outside and was asking Carol questions about pay and requirements to be a caregiver. Suddenly, we both heard a blood-curdling scream from inside the house. I ran inside as fast as possible and yelled, "I'm right here, I'm right here." Donna had finished her soup and was alone in the house when she got up from the table. I grabbed and held her in my arms to comfort her, apologizing repeatedly. I was wrong. I knew it. As I was outside talking, I knew I was taking too long to talk. I kept thinking I was taking too long but didn't say anything to Carol as she was answering my questions. We were probably only talking for 8 minutes, but I broke my rules of checking on her every five minutes. I broke down crying after Carol left, having caused Donna fear and anguish. She was crying, too, and apologized for yelling. She felt she had made me cry and was sorry. I told her it was my fault, not hers. You never know what will cause confusion leading to fear and panic in a person with Alzheimer's.

I want to interject something here. This incident happened seven years into Donna's illness, yet she had the wherewithal to apologize. She is still herself, a humble person, and her love for me is still there to the point where she doesn't want to hurt me.

A couple of times, Donna accused me of having another woman in the house. Both times she was with me, when she thought a woman was making advances towards me right there in our living room. At first, I couldn't figure out what she was talking about. I told her there was no one else in the room, but she heard the woman make a pass at me. That's when I looked at the TV. We were watching a movie, and the scene at that moment was a man and a woman dancing at a party. The actress was flirting with the star of the film. Donna couldn't differentiate between what was real and what was on the TV. The other time this happened, I was in the bathroom shaving with the radio on. She heard this woman talking and thought the lady was in the bathroom with me. As it turned out, it was the D.J. on the radio.

Although Donna needs constant reassurance of my love for her, I can tell she knows it even if I don't say it. For my part, I do as I've always done. I tell her every day that I love her. Anyway, I must learn to forget these incidents as fast as she does. I got angry because she couldn't accept there was no one there and I was with her, but she eventually did. I can't wake up still sore the next day as I've done when we've argued at night. My ego must let it go because she usually has forgotten everything in the morning. That's why I've called this book "Alzheimer's: A Caregiver's Journey into Love". As time passes, I must swallow my pride and love with an unselfish love. My ability to love her from my heart instead of from my mind is a slowly learned lesson for someone as selfish as I used to be. But I must tell you that the decision to love unconditionally is a daily decision for a caregiver of an Alzheimer's patient. It's too bad that we can't see that this attitude of loving unconditionally applies to marriages, also. The scripture says, "There's no greater love than to lay down your life for another!" Imagine if married couples started knowing that they are just beginning to learn about love rather than thinking this falling-in-love infatuation will last a lifetime. Imagine deciding daily to work on a friendship that will last a lifetime. You might say it's impossible to accept someone at face value instead of trying to mold your partner into who you think they should be while refusing to give up your pride and self-centeredness. When you're a caregiver, you have two choices: to grow in love and patience or to wait idly as your relationship disintegrates. Yes, your partner is losing their mind, but I know that Donna loved me until she passed. I was her everything; she depended on me for support and encouragement through all her trials. If only married couples could see this. If I had seen from the beginning of our marriage how important Donna was to me and how she would be taken away from me, maybe I would have been less selfish. But, of course, that's what life's experiences teach us. And that's what Alzheimer's was teaching me.

One night, on the way home from Toastmaster's public speaking meeting with Donna, I pulled over on the off-ramp of the freeway to help a couple of ladies change a flat tire. I left her in the car by herself. It took a while to swap out the regular tire for the spare, and by the time I got back to Donna, she was crying and yelling because she was strapped in with her seat belt, and I was gone. It was dark; she was alone, and fear and imagination took over. When changing the tire, I knew I should check on her, but I didn't follow my instincts. Again, I was wrong, and I felt horrible. Not thinking ahead and anticipating possibilities isn't cutting it anymore. These were just two examples of me causing fear and panic to her that never should have happened. In both cases, I knew better. I felt inside I should check on her and push those feelings aside. You've heard it before, we've all heard it before, "follow your instincts"! If something is telling you inside something isn't right, those are red flags. As a caregiver, you must follow those feelings, not ignore them. Again, it's like taking care of a child. They depend on you. They count on you being there when they need you. I know many inconveniences being a caregiver, but choosing to be a caregiver means denying yourself and laying down 'your life' for the person you are caring for. I don't say this lightly. Most caregivers taking care of family members were forced into it by circumstances. Whether the reason is financial or there is no one else to do it. But by taking on that responsibility, you have chosen an act of love. You may even hate the person because you have been put in this position. Yet when you hear of someone else doing this, you think what love they have! If you can see within yourself, you too are committing an act of love, then maybe you can comfort yourself with the knowledge you have a 'purpose,' you have a 'calling.' Your suffering and sacrifice are helping that person get through their suffering. It's not easy. At times, it's 'hell on earth'. Give yourself credit for being a special person because many have just walked away. Instead of being angry, love yourself enough to push through another day. Love yourself enough to get yourself help. Whether you believe it or not, you can't do it alone. Some government agencies help, like the Alzheimer's Association. Friends, family, or churches are the first places to look. More than anything, you can reach out to God like I did. Prayer is a powerful tool. Meditation is also a way to calm your anxieties. I'm very hyper, and it's hard for me to meditate for long periods. But I've found even a few minutes at a time helped me. Just breathing deeply and slowly by itself helps in the moment.

One evening, we sat on the couch, and she said she had to go somewhere. She was pointing out in front of herself while she was talking. Finally, I got it; she had been in this room and that room, and now she wanted to go into the bedroom because she was tired and wanted to go to bed. Another night, after Donna had gone to bed, I remember thinking I live in the 'Twilight Zone.' Nothing will ever be the same again. We live in a world of our own. Not just two people who want to live away from everyone else but live an existence far from the 'normal' everyday life others have. Our world has its rules, playing field, and perceptions, and trying to reconcile both is like trying to compare Picasso's paintings with Normal Rockwell. Everyone struggles in life, but communication is the difference between overcoming and handling the situation. We discuss it if we're over budget or if the car breaks down, and we communicate to the mechanic what the symptoms are. When a child disobeys, we explain the wrong and why things should be done a certain way. All of life is communication, and in the world of Alzheimer's patients, that 'normal' communication system no longer has any significance. We deal in puzzles and riddles, and the Caregiver is playing a constant game of charades, hoping there is enough of the picture to respond to the patient's needs in a way that reduces their frustration. Hoping to enhance their quality of life a little better today than yesterday, we stretch and strain our minds, attempting to learn and understand just one more gesture and facial expression that will give us a direction to go, a course to follow.

Communication is the key to any relationship. If a married couple wants to survive their marriage, make it last, they must open up themselves and communicate. It's the same in friendship or business or a parent-child relationship. It's not the same, though, with an Alzheimer's patient. Communication gains today may not be there tomorrow. Understanding behaviors today may mean nothing next week or next month. You work together in the first few years to get the point across and experience frustrations. As time passes, disappointment becomes a daily battle for the caregiver when the patient can no longer be a part of a solution. The caregiver is left holding the bag. This is when the disease is an avalanche of decline that no one can stop.

Of course, it's heart-wrenching to watch your spouse or parent or grandparent go through this because you know it will only get worse. But we must never forget that two people are in this relationship. My friend Ed said he makes it a point to come by at least twice a week to see me because he can't imagine what it would be like for me when Donna can't talk. We've been friends for over four years, and he's seen the progression of the disease with my wife. There is no way to measure the importance of what he's doing for me. Imagine how much it means to know you have someone consciously planning part of their week around your needs. I have many friends, and anyone who has been a caregiver knows you must have an outlet to get a break from a patient and have someone to talk to. Ed and I talk about politics or the stock market; neither of us cares to push each other's opinions on each other. It's talk, and that's all it's meant to be. Once we've solved the problems of the world and had a cup of my lousy coffee, Ed leaves until the next time, and I've had a much-needed little break from the daily routine. How blessed I was to have my other friends Dave and Sammy and Jimmy and Dan, who also came by regularly to spend time with me over coffee. Donna usually watched TV at this time during these morning visits. Another example of her awareness is when my friends and I talked. If we said something funny, Donna would bust out laughing. She was listening to us as well as the television.

This one day, Donna had a real scare. Something in her mind was evil and frightened her. At the time, I was at work. Later, I asked her if Annie helped, and she said no, Annie had her stuff to do. This isn't a negative reflection against Annie. She was probably in her room, and Donna wouldn't bother her. That's the kind of person Donna was her whole life. After work, we talked about what happened. That's when I had to explain to Donna that Alzheimer's is making her hallucinate. I tried to explain to her in simple terms what was happening to her brain, even though I didn't want to. I quietly told her nothing could be done outside of God healing her. She said, "I'm just going away."

CHAPTER 3

She's Up Again

She's up again! And wants to go somewhere or do something I can't figure out. It's 12:30 a.m. This isn't a disease; it's a flipping nightmare. She won't go to bed and doesn't want to sit up. Getting enough sleep is hard when you must stay up past midnight to get time alone. I forced her verbally to sit until she figured out what she wanted to do. That's when I put on a videotape of Joyce Meyers and sat silently beside her. Donna and I had watched and listened to Joyce Meyers's preaching, which was encouraging and uplifting, especially for women, for years. I'm letting her talk to herself and just listen to the tape. Well, it's been over half an hour, and slowly, she forgot what was on her mind that she couldn't figure out. She's getting too tired to remember what she was trying to do. She's listening to Joyce, and this is distracting her thinking. I also gave her a sleeping pill. I wouldn't say I like to do that because they don't usually work, but hopefully, being so late it will work. It's already 1 a.m. It infuriates me when she goes to bed and gets back up 5 minutes later, saying she never got anything to eat. I said, "I just fed you!" "Yeah, but I didn't get any." "I just fed you!". "Yeah, but I didn't get any." "Ok, get up and eat, get up; I fed you, but get up and eat!" Of course, she feels my anger, and I see that in her face. I must tell myself, 'It doesn't matter if you just fed her, let her get up and eat.' So, I got her a piece of cake I had bought her. The quote I have on the wall comes to mind. "Once dementia is diagnosed, the patient is excused 100% of the time!" She forgot my anger by the time she finished eating. I got it out of my system by writing it in my journal. I gave her a hug and a kiss.

She's listening to my tape about business while I finish the dishes. Letting the anger go as quickly as possible would be best. You have to have instant forgiveness. The scripture says, 'Love does not keep a record of wrong.' I've always thought of this scripture as forgetting things that have happened in the past. Yet when you are a caregiver, ignoring a record of wrong can be every hour. Patience isn't just a virtue; it's a way of life when you're a caregiver. And it doesn't happen overnight just because you read in a book to have patience. It's so easy to take offense at the negative behavior as if it's directed at me. Her anger and frustration are often directed at me because I'm the person who's there. Yet I continually remind myself she's not making a personal attack on me; she's got to be allowed to get her anger and frustration out of her system.

She's not making up her state of mind; instead, she's trying to figure it out, with a sense that it doesn't work right anymore. I look forward to Donna going to bed at night so I can have some time alone. It's 'my' time. Just a little quiet time when I can read or write. Maybe I'll watch a little TV, but not often that late. It's a time when I have no caregiving responsibilities, just for a few minutes. Not that I don't have things to do, like dishes or laundry. But man, I lose my patience so quickly with her because most nights, she goes to bed dead tired, and as soon as she lays down, her mind wakes up. Suddenly, something isn't right, and she can hardly tell me what it is. If she has something on her mind, it doesn't matter if I give her a sleeping pill; she lays there and gets up five times trying to figure out something she can't tell me or figure out. I try to keep her up as long as she stays awake, but she finally will go to bed alone or fall asleep on the couch.

For me, as I'm writing in my journal, I see that it is my selfishness that makes me impatient. It's my expectation as to how the evenings were supposed to play out. And when it doesn't go like I want it to, then I'm the one who gets frustrated and angry. When I must get up every few minutes to solve a problem that doesn't exist, I let it get to me. You must realize a caregiver's day starts early and sometimes ends late. I'm always tired, and the more tired I am at night, the harder it gets for me to be patient. Like one night, she was trying to tell me she had to do something and kept pointing to the bathroom. As it turned out, her back was itching. I remember thinking, 'When you ask God to show you and teach you how to serve others, He will answer your prayer. Probably not in the way you would expect. Being a caregiver will undoubtedly lead you to humility. Teach you of a love that begins when you've run out of energy and strength and carries you through another day. Another time, Donna was sitting on the couch and saying she had to go somewhere. I told her you are home; this is where you live. The third time, she said I've been here and here (pointing out to herself). Finally, I got it. She just wanted to go to bed in the other room, but again, in a short time, she got up again. It got to the point where I was upset again. She apologized, "I'm sorry I'm this way." The second time she got up, she could feel my frustration. Even after years of Alzheimer's, she is still there enough to apologize.

It truly is hard, though, to get enough sleep. I settle with the fact I'm so tired when I go to sleep that I sleep soundly for a few hours. There's a point though, where the caregiver never catches up with rest. I often notice I'm tired from the lack of sleep and mental exhaustion. I remember writing in my journal, 'There's a lot of good happening in our lives, but I'm just so depressed. It's so true: God is my strength. I have no strength of my own. I can't give up. If I don't keep pushing forward, I'll die. If I stop looking ahead and planning for a future purpose, my depression will overcome me. Jesus is my hope, my strength, and my salvation. I wrote this when my wife was in the seventh year of disease. I didn't know we still had seven more years to go. I live for Donna now. I don't care about anything for myself. My mind is so occupied with her I don't feel like going to the dentist to keep up with my dental care. I don't care if I eat right as long as she's fed. I can't pay attention to both our needs. I remember reading that many caregivers die before their patients because they don't care for themselves. Finally, at that time, Donna's doctor, Dr. Collier, switched her medicine to Zyprexa. This completely changed everything. She was tired all the time, but this was one behavior swapped for the others. It was so much better for Donna and I. I was running out of patience at night, and this medicine helped Donna sleep better, which changed our situation.

This worked for a while, but I didn't like how she was 'drugged.' I read in 'The Alzheimer's Solution,' how people over-medicate their patients so they don't have to deal with their behavior. And I realized that even though by that time I had cut the dosage of Donna's medicine in half so she shouldn't be overly doped up or tired at night, I still wait for her to go to bed. My emotions are so mixed up in this situation. I wait all day at work to be off to hurry home and be with her.

When I'm not with her, I miss being with her. Yet, on my days off, I revert to waiting for her to go to bed. No matter how much you love someone, caring for them 24/7 wears you out. You might think, 'Don't you get a break when you go to work?' not at all. At work, my mind Is focused on Donna. 'How is she doing?' 'Is she safe?' 'Does she remember I'm at work right now?' Again, I'm so thankful I live close enough to work that I can rush home for a few minutes on my lunch hour to let her know I'm nearby. It takes about 15 minutes to get home, so I have at least a half hour to spend with her. I fix lunch for us, and after we've eaten, it's time for me to return to work. Fortunately, the second half of my shift is usually shorter than the first, so it doesn't seem long before I'm done. For instance, if I go in at 7 a.m., my lunch is usually 1 or 2 p.m., then off at 4. At the time Dr. Collier gave Donna the medicine Zyprexa, she was hallucinating and confused a lot and not sleeping well. Zyprexa is what they call a 'black box' medicine. It's an anti-psychotic drug with a 2-4% chance of causing death. Some of the side effects are stroke, muscle spasms, and tiredness. At first, it was worth exchanging behaviors because she was calmer and tired, which helped with sleep. But that didn't last long. Her muscle spasms and doped-up behavior weren't my wife, so I couldn't let it go on.

This was just one major decision that made me think of the future. I wasn't looking forward to the hard choices I saw coming for me. Not just about medicine but how long I could care for Donna at home, even with the help of caregivers. I hate the idea of her going into a home. Donna's psychiatrist, Dr. Wright, was accommodating and supportive. He was always willing to discuss different options, and I was very comfortable with the actions we were taking.

I want to point out that my decisions weren't made alone. After Donna couldn't talk or think straight, all decisions about her life were mine to make. This is not easy, especially when no other family members are involved. Yet I didn't make any decision without counsel. I had my wife's doctors to discuss everything with. Her physicians were, at first, Dr. Macias. Being female, she helped me understand female issues. Dr. Collier, who came later, helped with the meds and disease issues. We had Dr. Wright and a couple of different neurologists. Once we started getting caregivers, we had our case worker, Terry P., also a caregiver for her family member. Her counsel was invaluable. Eventually, when Donna went into the home, the manager, Becky, became almost like a mentor for me. She had years of experience taking care of patients with life-threatening diseases. Which, of course, Alzheimer's is.

In her caregiver's workbook, 'Am I My Parent's Keeper,' author Cosette Riggs states empathetically, "Do Not Minimize the Problems of Taking Personal Care of a Dependent Parent." For me, it was my spouse. This statement is precisely why I sought out counsel from everyone I knew or came in contact with who had any experience with Alzheimer's or dementia or had been a caregiver of anyone with a life-threatening disease. I want to take you back to a comment I made in chapter one that exemplifies Mrs. Rigg's point. I had mentioned that my wife, of 24 years, had false teeth. Never in our marriage, until her hip replacement in 2006, had I seen her without her teeth. Never had I seen her or anyone else in my life use denture cream to align their dentures. In truth, you could say I 'minimized' the problem of denture care back in 2006. Donna was just two years into her diagnosis and could continue aligning her dentures after her hip operation. It didn't enter my mind to have her explain how to use the denture cream on her teeth and get it right while doing it. That would have been the perfect time to ask her to show me because I had already seen her with her teeth out. I didn't, though. This minimizing of the problem caused Donna and I much anguish later on. When using a denture cream, you squeeze the tube of cream onto the denture plate in a line that doesn't completely cover the denture but enough so that it securely 'glues' the denture to the top or bottom of the mouth. After applying the cream, I had to put the teeth into her mouth so that the paste would spread out evenly in the right places. Then, I would remove the denture, check it, and put it back in her mouth.

I did this with the top and bottom plates. Now, imagine having a blindfold on while someone is sticking their hands in your mouth to remove your teeth or candy at the back of your mouth. Imagine having no idea what this person is doing to you, only they keep putting their hands in your mouth, trying to get something out or put something in. Donna couldn't see what I was doing. She no longer remembered the procedure to align her teeth. It was like I was trying to put my finger down her throat. It was uncomfortable and scary, and she didn't like it. From my perspective, this alignment had to be done right. Like most people, she relied on her teeth to eat. I had to learn by trial and error. There was one Sunday I fixed Donna's teeth, only I screwed them up. She couldn't wear the bottoms for two days. All I could feed her was soft foods. As I said before, I had never seen them out of her mouth until her hip replacement. Seeing her suffer from the pain she endured when they didn't fit right killed me. She was used to realigning her teeth every week. But it was getting harder and harder for her to take the process. I aligned them weekly for a while, but slowly, it became every two weeks, then three weeks, then eventually once a month. As the Alzheimer's worsened, she became more confused about what I was doing. She would pull back and fight me. It took me over an hour initially to do the job. As it began to take longer, the struggle for both of us became harder.

This struggle lasted for most of four years. It wasn't until she almost died in November 2013 that I took her dentures out for the last time. It aged her twenty years, but I had no choice when she recovered; I decided not to put her through the alignment process again. We had gone to a specialist to see if we could get her a new set of teeth. Once the dentist examined her, he said the only way for her to get new teeth was to rebuild her mouth. You see, she had had these dentures since she was 21. The dentures had worn down her bone structure over the years. There was no way I would make her go through that in her mental state. Neither did the dentist recommend it. Financially, we could have gotten the money. But a trauma like that would have pushed her even farther into her dementia.

As a new caregiver, it would benefit you to write down and list future tasks you may encounter. Again, an example list of care and legal decisions and home placement can be found in the Caregiver's workbook by Mrs. Riggs, a long with so many other topics a caregiver will need to know, things that are invaluable to a new caregiver. It's a big mistake to underestimate the extent of care a patient with Alzheimer's will need. Here are three entries from the caregiver Kathleen's daily log. (I made every caregiver record the daily activities and medicines given.) The first entry is from the day before I left for a trip to Visalia, California. I was meeting my friend Barry in Bakersfield to visit our high school buddy Kevin, who was dying from cancer. This trip would not have been possible if Kathleen had not agreed to stay with Donna for three days at our home. Her husband Brian would come to visit Kathleen at night. Thursday 2-16: (Kathleen's words) "We were sitting on the couch watching "The Cross." Shortly after we finished the movie, she became agitated and started panicking, saying, "I'm going to die." She was getting out of control. She stood up crying, and I held her and asked her to look me in the eye. That gave her some focus. I held her and prayed out loud, and led her to her bed, where we both sat, and I continued to soothe her. She relaxed and laid down and slept for ½ hour. When she awoke, she acted as if it never happened. I did not tell Cam as I didn't want to alarm him. Kathleen was a special person; she cared for Donna and me both.

Friday 2-17: Kathleen's notes

"Cameron left at 4 a.m. today, heading for California for an overnight trip. I slept with Donna. At 7 a.m., she had her med & 2 tablespoons of mineral oil at 8:45 a.m. I gave her a suppository, and an hour later, she had a BM around 12:30 p.m., we went to my borrowed van to get the mail, and went to the lake. When getting in the van, she said, "Oh, I remember this." I guess she remembered getting into it previously. After getting the mail, we headed for the lake. I received an important phone call. When we reached the boat launch and stopped, I continued my conversation. Donna was getting agitated again. I finished my phone call, and Donna went into a full-blown frenzy. She again started with, "I'm going to die," then she pointed at the lake and inside the van, the dash, a yellow plastic bag for trash, talking gibberish. So, I got her out of the van and tried to get her to focus on my eyes like yesterday. Nothing worked; her eyes were glazed over, and she kept screaming as loud as she could and saying, "No, no, no," + "I'm going to die." At one point she quietly told me she was sick, meaning her mind. Most everything else she said I couldn't understand. So, I called Cameron, hoping that hearing his voice would calm her down. It didn't. She had a one-track mind, and it was driving her crazy. I got her back in the van, still with Cam on the phone. I went a short distance, but she was just out of control. So, I stopped and asked Cam for permission to give her ½ of 0.5 mg of Xanax. She wouldn't take it. I put it in her mouth and gave her H20. But she wouldn't take the water. I can only assume she swallowed it. I had to get Cam off the phone & get her home. She continued to be out of control, thrashing about and pulling her legs up. I held her arm while driving, trying to calm her. Finally, I said I would have to call an ambulance for her if she didn't stop. She would momentarily calm down, then start all over again. We went through this 3 x till we got home.

The Xanax was given to her approx. 1:30. At 1:50, we were home, and she calmed down but was still muttering –it appeared to me that she was perhaps hearing and answering voices. I honestly believe that this panic attack brought on hallucinations. At 3:50, she laid down and slept for 40 min. I could tell the worst was over, and she was exhausted. At 5:20, I laid her down again because she kept falling asleep on the couch. She got up in 2 min. She said she felt "woozy," I gave her a bar to eat. Not dinner, as she said she wasn't hungry. At 5:45 p.m., she continued to complain of not feeling well. I gave her three ibuprofen and laid down with her. She kept saying, "I'm sorry," + "I love you," then asked, "Where is Cam?" I told her and asked if she wanted to talk to him. She was affirmative, so I called him. She was lucid but exhausted. 6:50 p.m., we got up. I gave her hot tea and something to eat. Then, her med Namenda and melatonin. 10 p.m. 2 calms (over-the-counter relaxers from the Dollar Store) + 3 ibuprofen (for stiffness) and off to bed. No incidents all night.

Sat Feb 18th: Kathleen's notes.

We were in the kitchen by 7:30 a.m. 8:15 a.m. – med, vitamin & 1 tbs min oil 11 a.m. – 3 ibuprofen – for pain. Donna is very quiet but alert and answers & laughs appropriately when prompted. Around 1:30 p.m., we took a walk to Dave and Sharon's + visited briefly, then came home. We listened to music; I had a couple of phone calls. Approx. 3:30 p.m. Cam called. At first, Donna was happy to hear his voice. Then, as Cam repeatedly said he would be home tonight, when it was dark, etc., she became confused, and I had to end the call. She was starting to panic, mumbling something about dying. I needed to nip this in the bud, so before she was full blown into it, I gave her two calms @ 3:50 p.m. And took her to bed and lay with her. We napped until 4:30. It is now 5:35 pm, she has her dinner, but she needs reminding to eat. She does seem a bit confused and possibly somewhat depressed all day. 5:45 p.m. 1 tbs min oil, 7 p.m. med & melatonin, 8:30 p.m. 3 ibuprofen, 8:30 p.m. in bed, but soon up again, 10 pm we were headed for bed & Cam came home." (End Kathleen's notes).

On the first day of my trip, I had just met my friend Barry at a restaurant in Bakersfield when I got a call from Kathleen. Donna was so upset I had to leave the table and go outside to deal with the situation. I wasn't too happy with the interruption. It's almost impossible to deal with the problem at home over the phone. Besides the fact I was hoping to get a little break, it was uncomfortable sitting back down at the table with Barry when I was so upset. Yet there was nothing I could do except to explain the situation. Barry's mother was developing dementia at the time, so he understood. You can see from the entries Kathleen had written how much my wife's moods would change. The hallucinations had been going on for years when this trip was taken. Whether it was me or Donna's other caregivers, our patience was tested constantly. That is why it is so hard for caregivers to maintain their health physically and mentally. In my journal, I often expressed feeling like I was going insane. I would say, "I am insane; I am out of my mind!" It was a temporary feeling that I had to fight constantly. You can see that sometimes Donna was lucid. She loved to laugh; she was a sweet person. Nevertheless, the constant stress of figuring out what to do in the moment you're in would wear me out.

How can anyone possibly understand what it is like to see yourself and know you are losing your mind? And she knew what Alzheimer's was and where she was headed. She knew that as her constant companion, she depended on me, and it would take, in the end, a toll on me. She never worried about herself; she worried about me. She was still Donna. Most people said or thought she wasn't there anymore, but they were mistaken. Donna touched all her caregivers with her heart. She made others laugh right up until the end. Her inner being and spirit never changed because she had Alzheimer's disease. Even still, in human existence, the body was deteriorating and dying. But I beg to differ with those who believe she was gone. Her inner being and spirit never changed because she had Alzheimer's disease. Most people don't see what I saw.. Even still, 99% of the caregivers loved Donna. Her sweetness, humility, and sense of humor are not lost in the disease. Again, even in this sickness, we were blessed. I didn't go through the insanity of an "angry" person with Alzheimer's. Sure, Donna had a short period when she was angry most of the time. But this wasn't who she became. It was the result of the frustration she was going through. Many relatives dealt with the patients full of anger and hate until they died. This is another example of what Mrs. Riggs pointed out about not underestimating the patient's required care. I've had friends who went through their spouse's or a grandmother's change from a sweet person into a hateful, even violent individual. How can a caregiver not take it personally when your kind, considerate grandma cusses you out, out of nowhere, for no apparent reason? I was blessed because it was just a phase for Donna. After a time, she returned to her laughing, quiet self.

She accepted God's hand in this early on. She didn't question God, get angry at him, or lose her faith. Nevertheless, it didn't mean she didn't go through a horrible hell of frustration and confusion. In 2007, four years after diagnosis, Donna drew her last picture. It was so childlike compared to her pre-Alzheimer's ability, what she knew she was capable of, that she said she was done with drawing. You'll read or hear how you need to try and keep the patient doing what they loved before to keep their minds active. Alzheimer's patients can learn new things or relearn old stuff to a certain degree for a certain period; I tried to keep her interested in her art even if it wasn't the same or as good as in the past. She remembered her past works and couldn't accept what she'd become. As I get older, I get frustrated not being able to do the physical things I once could or remember things like I used to. Amplify that frustration by 10 or 100 times. That's what your relative is going through. Donna loved playing games. She loved doing crossword puzzles and playing scrabble. I'm pretty sure I beat her once or maybe twice in all the years we played. It was cause for a big celebration. She was so good at doing crossword puzzles she made up her own. And that wasn't all she created. She created a Christian game to help new Christians grow in the 'Word.' Here, I must make a confession that I bet most husbands could make if they were honest. My wife was a very talented person. She had her dreams.

Nevertheless, men tend to think that her dreams are set aside when we get married, and our goals are number one. A marriage is supposed to be a partnership where you complement, support, and encourage each other. That form of love I was lacking in until I became a caregiver. I can't say I never put her desires over mine. I supported her in what she did. When she was involved in a prison ministry in Tucson through our church, I got involved, too. I didn't stick with it like she did. When we taught a bible study at home, we both taught it. Donna would naturally reach out to younger or older women in our group. We worked together on some products when we made and sold crafts in Colorado. I confess that I treated her gifts and accomplishments as hobbies, but my dreams were serious; I was going to change the world. Over and over, I would want something for one of my projects, like learning keyboards. Donna bought me a Casio electric keyboard to learn so I could do my music. Thirty-five years later, I still haven't learned that keyboard. When she made up a game, we played it with others. They liked it, but instead of investing in getting it made, I let it sit on the shelf. It would have been worth the investment that would have been necessary to get it produced. At least two times, we had the money to accomplish this but didn't, whereas when I wanted to invest money, oh, it was so important. I guess it's a cultural thing. "I'm the man, the head of the household". Christian men tend to forget the scriptures that say, 'Husbands love your wives, just as Christ loved the church and gave himself up for her.' (Ephesians 5:25 NIV). We forget that when the Bible was written, they had a totally different culture in the Middle East than we do today. Women then didn't have the freedom that they have today. But if you understand the culture, it didn't mean they weren't treated with the highest respect by men who knew what true love was.

I mentioned in chapter two we were living in the Twilight Zone, but by now, I was out of my mind. Life for me was completely insane. There are no rules, as Jackson Browne sang, I'm running on empty.' If it weren't for work, I wouldn't remember one day from the next. I felt constantly like I was forgetting something. There was always something in the back of my mind. I felt like it would eventually come together, but in the meantime I was barely hanging on. If you were hired as a caregiver for a family member, you would have no history with the patient and nothing to take personally by the patient's behavior. One of the reasons caregiving is so difficult for family members is that we take the behavior personally. We remember how the person used to be. We feel sorry for ourselves. We set ourselves up for disappointment by not allowing the person who has Alzheimer's to be themselves. They were not who we wanted them to be, not who they were last month, week, yesterday, or even an hour ago. Who they are this minute is what matters. It's so interesting that people join religions, study meditation, read books, learn to live in the 'now,' and be present. With Alzheimer's, you are forced to live in the now. To survive as a caregiver, I must let go of yesterday and have no expectations for tomorrow. Instead, I must learn to live in the moment of today. The last hour was an evil hour, redirecting their focus. This hour was happy; treasure it while it lasts.

I was reading the book 'Illusions' by Richard Bach. He said having been a flight instructor, he knew that students tend to make easy things complicated. It made me realize that caregivers are students learning to be caregivers. And he was right. For many years, I made things more complex than they needed to be. It says in the Bible, "he that increases knowledge increases sorrow." (Ecclesiastes 1:18). That's the way it is with Alzheimer's disease. The more I studied and learned, the more it hurt to know what would happen. However, I still believe that family members who are caregivers should read as much as they can and watch television specials on caregiving for an Alzheimer's patient. When I first started reading books about Alzheimer's, I seldom got through three-quarters of the books. I didn't want to read about the end, the final stage. I regretted that later on. I didn't want to think about what Donna would go through. I didn't want to accept what I would have to go through. I returned and finished the books, but I wished I had done it sooner. The more knowledge you have, the better prepared you will be for each stage of your journey, giving you strength and understanding to make it through.

Depending on what study or book you read, there could be three stages, seven steps, or ten of Alzheimer's. Different scientist describes the progress differently. I think one of the things to understand is that the stages aren't cut and dry. You could say Donna was two-thirds of the way through one step and beginning to show signs of the next step. It's not like school moving from grades one to two and three. The stages run together. I remember more than once realizing two months or so after the fact she had moved to a new level of the disease. No two people are going to go through this the same. And that's true of caregivers as well. I often had to remind myself how much Donna loved me and how much I loved her. It's true that I also spent many nights crying partially because I was worn out and depressed. But mostly because I was losing my partner, my best friend.

I spent many hours by myself taking care of Donna over the 14 years she had Alzheimer's, but boy, how wrong I'd be if I didn't acknowledge the fantastic support I received from all the caregivers Donna had. There's no way I can comment on every caregiver that helped us. Once we qualified for Arizona Long Term Care, we had many caregivers. Some came for only a day, some for a few days, and some for weeks, although not every day. Looking back at the daily log,

I see the names of the ladies who assisted us, and there were many. I can't comment on everyone except to say that they all took good care of Donna. Sure, some only did the minimum required, but most read to Donna, watched TV with her, cooked for her, and made her laugh when they could. I think only one complained and quit over all the years because Donna slapped her hand. And there was only one I had to fire. Mostly, they all liked Donna because she was a sweet person inside. Yet there were a few who I wanted to single out. These ladies went above and beyond, and some just because they volunteered their free time to give me a break.

First, Sandy C. and Jan K. were both ladies we knew from church. They both were a little older than us. Both would come over for a couple of hours to give me a break to go grocery shopping or to have coffee with a friend. This was voluntary, and I didn't have to pay for them. You can't imagine how precious those ladies were to me. They, at the time, would come separately once a week. I looked forward to these days because I didn't have much other help then. To get out for those two hours was a God send. I made sure Donna was fed and changed before either one showed up. They would watch TV with Donna or sit in the living room and read their book if she was asleep when they came. I was never more than 15 minutes away if there was a problem or Donna needed to be changed. They would call me, and I'd come; I will always be grateful for their help.

I mentioned before our first regular caregiver, Annie. Annie moved in with us in October 2010 while going through a divorce. It worked out for both of us because we traded caregiving for rent. As with most Filipina women I've met through caregiving, Annie is humble and quiet. She has the heart of a servant. I was still working, and to have someone to give of herself freely to Donna gave me peace when I went to work every day. And she was an excellent companion to Donna, and she cooked for her in the evening, or for all of us. Also, she helped me with cleaning. Words cannot express what a benefit Annie was to us at a time when I had no money to afford a caregiver and still was working full-time––another example of how God blessed us through a horrible disease. "Maraming Salamat" Annie.

Kathleen was the second person to help us for an extended period. Kathleen was another special person who had the heart of a servant. It was in the summer of 2010 that I first met Kathleen. I needed another caregiver. I needed someone to help and give Annie a break, so I called our church. First Baptist of Williams and asked them to put out a notice to the church that I needed help. It wasn't long before I got a call from a woman in Hawaii. Kathleen introduced herself and said that she heard about our needs. She was visiting her daughter, Elizabeth, in Hawaii, who was having a baby. Kathleen told me she and her husband Brian had recently moved to Williams and were looking for part-time work. I told her I needed a caregiver but couldn't afford to pay her. Not exactly the position she was looking for. She said she'd have to pray about it. I didn't expect to hear from her again. It was about a week later, I received a call from Kathleen. I think she was back in Williams by then. She said she felt God was telling her to take the position even though I offered no pay. A stranger was willing to work for free for someone she didn't even know——another example of God blessing us through our trials. Kathleen started working one day a week. This gave Annie a well-needed break. In all, I think Kathleen helped us for around three years. In 2012, when we began receiving Arizona Long Term Care, they paid 30 hours a week for caregivers. We then were able to help Kathleen get hired by one of the caregiving companies. She then got training and started getting paid for taking care of Donna. Through this time, we became friends with Kathleen and her husband, Brian. Once in a while, Kathleen would cook for all four of us. Brian would come to our house after work, and when I got home, we'd all eat together with Donna. I want to share a letter that Kathleen wrote concerning Donna. "I first met Donna 6 months ago. Since then, it has been my pleasure to give her caregiver and husband some respite time at least once a week. From the very beginning, I felt a bond with Donna. She has a certain charm about her. Then, her husband, Cameron, left a booklet of poems on the table to read. Donna wrote everything. Reading these poems showed me more of the lovely inner person of her being. She is one special lady, and I am so glad to play a part in her life. Can you say that I love Donna? I so do!!!"

How blessed we were to have Kathleen as a caregiver and how lucky we were to be friends with her and Brian.

Tammy was another caregiver who stood out. She was a person who didn't like to sit around. Tammy was Donna's caregiver on more than one occasion. At least twice, she helped us for extended periods. She did more than feed Donna and watch TV with her. Whenever Donna was watching a movie by herself or sleeping, Tammy cleaned. Please understand caregivers have guidelines for what needs to be done or accomplished during the day. All the caregivers cooked for Donna and changed her when needed. But imagine how surprised and delighted I was to come home and find Tammy had washed out the cupboards or washed the windows. Not only did I not have time for much extra cleaning, but it wasn't exactly high on my priority list.

Extra stuff like this made me so grateful for her help. It would be like a single mother coming home from work, and the babysitter had vacuumed, done the dishes, and cleaned the bathrooms. No words can truly express what that does for the single mom or the husband of an Alzheimer's spouse. Donna's journey, our journey, was made so much easier because of caregivers.

CHAPTER 4

38 Dollars in the Bank

When Donna's aunt Bobbi first sent me "The Story," I thought 'Why are you sending this to me?' It wasn't like I didn't love my wife or I was going to abandon her. I think I was trying to decide if I should be offended. I couldn't decide, so I put the thought on hold. Kind of like, 'Well, I'm not sure how to take this, so I'll wait on my decision.' At the time, Donna had only been diagnosed for a while; if anything, it was too early to think of the issue. But as time went on, it became more and more evident how important the story and its point were. Sure, it's easy to say initially that I'll stick it through to the end no matter what. In the front, you have absolutely no idea of the journey you are about to embark on. How many runners at the starting line of their first 26-mile marathon think, 'I am in shape; I can handle this.' Halfway through, they start thinking, 'Man, I'm only halfway through; how am I ever going to make it to the end?' And, of course, so many of them indeed drop out, but some push on, saying to themselves, 'I can't quit; I've come too far!'

The story is of a man visiting the nursing home daily to see his wife. Finally, the nurse asked him 'Why do you come here every day; she doesn't even know who you are?' His response to her, 'Yeah, but I know who she is.' At the time, my 'marathon' was just beginning. The trials hadn't even hardly begun. Sure, eventually, she forgot I was her husband, but she knew I was her caregiver. She knew I loved her. But the most important part, she, inside, was still who she was. A loving, caring, sweet, humble person with a sense of humor. It is written, "Love Suffers Long and is Kind., How important this act of love has to be practiced. No matter how much I thought I loved Donna, in truth I never knew what true love was before I became her caregiver. I can't deny the truth of the kind of person I was the first half of our marriage. I was a selfish and self-centered man. There are a lot of men like me, the old me. We have this chauvinistic attitude that what we want is all that matters. But through all this, Donna's Christian love for me never wavered. I've always said it, and it hasn't changed; my wife was the best example of Christ I've ever seen or experienced. Her love for me was more than I deserved; her forgiveness was beyond measure. Again, it is written, 'no greater love has a man than to lay down his life for a friend' (John 15:13 paraphrased). Donna did this for me; now, it was my turn to pay it forward.

I didn't start this journey with Alzheimer's thinking I would learn to love through this. Love was the last thing on my mind. For Donna and I, it was more like, how will we get through this? We were both terrified, but inwardly, we also knew that Christ was with us. To learn the love of God, a person must go through many trials and tribulations. It's a lot like the journey of financial success. Many entrepreneurs will tell you, many first attempts at a new business or idea fail. You must be willing to get back up, brush off the setback, and continue pushing toward your goal. Only those who give up and quit have failed. It's the same process in a marriage and the same road when dealing with Alzheimer's. Over and over, I must push through the anguish of frustration and misunderstanding of what I was going through. Time after time, I had to swallow my pride and let love be the power that got me through. I knew the sacrifices, goals, and desires Donna set aside years ago to love me as I was back then. That motivation pushed me to never give up on her now! I get a lot of praise for caring for Donna and sticking it out to the end. I fully know that many husbands or wives abandon their spouses when this situation happens in their marriages. I fully believe that when a spouse, child, brother, sister, or friend takes on the caregiving job, they should receive credit and appreciation for their actions. But it does not mean that that person is perfect or didn't make mistakes. How could I not make mistakes when dealing with situations that most men never encounter in their whole lives? For instance, others know how important it is to a baby to keep its bowels moving regularly. They know it's dangerous for a child to be constipated for too long. They know how sick a baby can get if it has diarrhea for too long. Suddenly, I'm no longer just my wife's companion but her mother. Constipation was a constant struggle during this disease. I learned about laxatives, suppositories, prune juice, and mineral oil. I had to make sure Donna drank enough water, ate the right foods, and had plenty of fiber in her diet. I learned the value of magnesium, and I learned how to give enemas. But all this didn't always solve the problem of constipation. When a patient has been constipated for too long, they get impacted. When Donna hadn't had a bowel movement in a few days, and we couldn't see the doctor immediately, I Googled what the doctor would have to do in this situation. It was a procedure that would be extremely painful for my wife. But as it turns out, it was also something I could do myself.

It was love and necessity that made me do it. I'm pretty sure I only had to take care of that problem one other time. I had to come to a place of understanding of who I had become. My roles in this movie, this nightmare, were many. I was this adult child's husband, doctor, nurse, friend, mother, and playmate. It wasn't necessary in the end to put her through the stress of getting her dressed to go outside in the cold. I would have to lift her into the van, then go to the emergency room and wait in a waiting room full of people, her not knowing what was happening. Whether I liked it or not, whether it grossed me out or not, does not matter anymore. What matters most is the care for your patient, what's most important for their best interest. This is where the learning of true love for another person is learned. Too often, all we see is the 'sacrifice' we or someone else makes and miss out on the blessing of knowing what we are becoming. Please don't misunderstand; hell is hell when you're going through it. But if you can strengthen your faith with words from others who have gone through it in your quiet moments, there is hope. You can and will make it through this. All too often, it's easy to cry to God, 'Why is this happening to us? We don't deserve this.' When suffering through events that are not your fault, the question is no longer why but rather where do we go from here? What is required of me today?

That wasn't the only trial by fire I endured. Diarrhea created another whole dilemma that I never would have imagined. I would have to deal with it in my caregiving experience—this time, I had to learn how to use a douche.

Humility raises his stern hand sometimes, and love anew is learned. At first, when I went to the stores to buy adult depends and douche and baby wipes, my pride and male ego were humbled and silenced real fast. Whether my pride was offended or not, I had to take care of her needs and 'love her.' I've seen in my life where pride goeth before the fall' and I hurt others. My wife depended on me, pride be damned. As it says in 1 Corinthians 13, love is not proud. Love always protects, always preserves. The act of love she received was for me to serve her. The act of love I received from God was to learn humility. I'm not perfect, and my conduct wasn't always excellent, but in life no one lives up to their own or other's expectations. Yet that doesn't change how much I loved Donna and how this whole experience has taught me what true love is. The best description I've ever read of love is I Corinthians 13. If a caregiver can set this as their standard to live by when taking care of someone else, they will learn to do these things in the long run of their experience. We usually don't start that way in a marriage or a caring relationship. But you will learn how to do these things if you persist, don't quit, don't give up. Sometimes, our own 'mind talk' brings us down. And, of course, this drains us of the energy we already don't have. Like I said before, I listened to audiobooks and sermons and read self-help books. My self-talk was so negative it took me, in my opinion, eight years to change my way of thinking. However, she had Alzheimer's for 14 years; I needed the extra strength for those last five years that my change of mindset gave me. I became grateful for the time Donna and I had together. I became thankful for all the help I received. I became grateful for the financial blessings we received. I learned to love Donna more profoundly than ever through this Alzheimer's experience. Let me tell you though, I wouldn't trade this experience for anything. Not for a minute do I regret this time with Donna for anything. I learned to give her more love and received love from her. She didn't remember me as her husband, but there is no doubt that she loved me and appreciated me taking care of her. Sacrificial love isn't what I did but rather what I learned.

I started studying motivational books and success literature back in 2003. My son Ryan had given me a book by Robert Kiyosake, "Rich Dad, Poor Dad." The whole thing was about attitude in life told through the stories of his dad and his best friend's dad. But the basis of the book was their attitude towards money and being successful. That led me to other books like Napoleon Hill's "Think and Grow Rich" and Zig Ziglar's "See You at the Top." It wasn't money I needed most right then. It was the motivation to push on. All these authors were successful because, despite their struggles at the beginning of their careers, they overcame all of them and became successful. That was the kind of encouragement I needed. The most encouraging and motivational book I read was the one that gave me hope. It lifted my spirit when down and strengthened my faith when I was weak. The Bible was my daily companion. It opened my eyes to things beyond this life and showed me a love I had only seen in one person. Donna was my mentor when it came to receiving a love undeserved. No one showed me the traits of Christ, forgiveness, kindness, patience, and sacrifice, like her. All the time I studied these books, I thought I was developing a positive attitude in life that would help me be successful in business. But now I see it was the hand of God preparing me for a battle that would take all the courage, positive thinking, and motivation I could grasp to keep me going forward to a higher purpose than business will ever be. What more extraordinary privilege is there in life than to take care of someone else and help them get through a disease that they or you can't survive alone? I would be remiss if I didn't mention the value to my state of mind of reading Joel Osteen's book "Your Best Life Now." At that point in my life, struggling with depression, this also supplied much-needed encouragement.

It was in 2006 that I tried to bring that success that would get money to pay our bills into a reality. I followed Napoleon Hill's advice and committed everything to my goal. In 2005, the Real Estate market was booming. Without much schooling and having been a meat cutter my whole life, I thought, "Real estate is the way to go." If I were successful, I would have plenty of money to pay our bills. My meat manager at Safeway agreed with me. He'd give me time off to go to Real Estate School if I didn't quit before he could go to Real Estate School while I covered for him. It took three weeks to finish the school. I studied hard because it had been years since I had been in school. I was so grateful to God when I passed the State exam, the first time. My older brother told me it took him three times to pass the test. Many people had told me how hard it was, and believe me, I was a "c" student in school, so this little miracle lifted my spirits. After filling in for my manager for three weeks while he took the school and passed the test, I quit Safeway. I was, again, taking the advice of Napoleon Hill. I burned all the bridges behind me and sailed full speed into the storm.

As I've stated before, Williams is a small town, and because of the booming market, more prominent companies all sent agents to open Real Estate offices in town, a town of 4000. Before it was over, we had 60 Real Estate agents in Williams. I didn't have the experience or money for advertisement that those 'company agents' had. In my first year, I made 12,000 dollars net. It is not a lot of money, but it is average at the time for first-year agents. Of course, most of those agents were in alot bigger cities. I took a significant pay cut that year. There was another problem for me that I couldn't have predicted or prepared for at that point. 2006 began the floor falling out from under the Real Estate Market. By 2007, I had spent all our savings and was broke. Then, with my tail between my legs, I returned to Safeway and asked for a job as a meat cutter. Humbled but grateful to God, Safeway in Williams gave me a job. Before that, I had worked for Safeway in Flagstaff, 35 miles away. So now, I had a regular income and worked only 8 miles from my house. What a blessing in disguise this experience had become.

I could go home to check on and be with Donna for lunch every day. It didn't all turn out the way I had planned or hoped. I wasn't a total failure as a Real Estate agent, but the timing was wrong. I still didn't know how to pay Donna's future medical bills. The solution would come years later.

In the end, as her husband and caregiver, "What do I care why this Alzheimer's happened? Should I question God as to why or how? Will this comfort or ease any pain of living with the truth." I know all that that brings is more anguish. There are so many facets to being a caregiver and so much required of you that you must constantly work on your attitude. I spent the first six and a half years worrying about what to do and how to pay for care when the time came. I finally realized I had to snap out of it. Our time together is short; I need to appreciate it, be thankful for it, and cherish it. Secondly, I won't be able to do this if I'm constantly down. Worry robs you of your power to make it through the day. Alzheimer's is a day-by-day, hour-by-hour experience.

Donna, out of the blue one day, turned to her caregiver, Kathleen, and asked, "Where's Cam?" You might say, "What's the big deal about that?" You see, I didn't know she even remembered my name. It was May 3, 2010, six years after her original diagnosis.

There are times I think, "That's the stupidest question anyone could ask, "Does she remember you?" They know she has Alzheimer's, hell!!! What do you mean, does she still remember me?" It was a constant reminder of what I was going through and would continue to go through. It's almost like being at the edge of a deep, dense forest and knowing there's no other way to go. You have to go through it. Sure, you have a 'flashlight' (the books on Alzheimer's I read). But all I see are humongous tall pine trees looming over me, shadowing any light from getting through. I have little idea where I'm headed or how, in heaven's name, I will get to the other side. I don't even know if there are any meadows of sunlight along the way. All I see is an arduously long journey ahead of me. All I wonder is, "Will Love and Faith sustain me?"

GRAND CANYON

Railway

Aug 7, 2008

CHAPTER 5

Precious Moments

In January of 2016, I was working a part-time job at Love's Truck Stop. I had been retired for two years, and Donna had been in the Ponderosa House Assisted Living Home for three years. It was April 19; I was notified that the Ponderosa House was closing down, and I had to find my wife another place to live. When Donna first got to the Ponderosa in 2013, she said she accepted that I was permanently putting her in a home. This was when I was still working at Safeway; she had only been in a wheelchair for a short while. In truth, it took her more than three months to adjust. We could tell because she would get angry and start yelling. There weren't any real reasons, but looking back, I could see frustration and anger at me leaving her there. I would visit twice a day if my work schedule allowed it. Donna and I would go out onto the front porch, and I would read the Bible to her. Then, if the weather permitted, we would walk around the block on the sidewalk. At the end of the block was a Mormon Church, and I would push Donna in her wheelchair over to their parking lot behind the church, and we would go all over the parking lot. We always had lots of fun doing this. Sometimes, I'd push her fast and act like a racer, and she would laugh. She loved to listen to oldies on my phone, only I picked out all the funny songs from the '50s, like 'Tie Me Kangaroo Down, Sport' by Rolf Harris. We would sing along, and I would exaggerate the funny parts. She loved to laugh and laugh at these songs. As often as possible, I would put Donna in the car and take her for a ride into the forest. We would go every day if I didn't work too late that day and the weather was good. As we were driving, I'd point out any deer I saw, and there were always geese at the golf course. As time went on, though we would pass the animals before she could even see them. The fact is the wildlife was more for me. They gave me something to look for along the way. I played music she remembered from the 50's and 60's. Being born in 1948, this was the music she grew up with. Donna just loved music. She introduced me to people like Nina Simone, Miriam Makeba, Ian Matthews, and Tim Buckley, and she loved Gordon Lightfoot. She always made me laugh when she played music at home. She would get out a record and play her favorite song, then switch to another album. Seldom did she ever play the whole album. (This was before Alzheimer's came into the picture).

It was while she was at the Ponderosa House in November of 2013 that Donna almost died. I went to see her around 5 p.m. that night. She seemed out of it. The caregiver said she had given her some medicine earlier because she was agitated. I liked the caregivers who were filling in at the house while the regular caregivers were on vacation to the Philippines to see family. It's a mother-and-daughter team. The mother is by the book on everything, and that is good. I have a lot of respect for her. Anyway, while taking Donna to bed, I stopped in the hallway to say hello to a couple of patients, Jerry and Richard, in the bedroom across from Donna's room, as was my habit. I turned back to push Donna into her bedroom, but she leaned forward in her wheelchair and fell straight to the floor. There was nothing I could do. Her wheelchair was in the doorway, and I couldn't get to her before she fell. She fell right on her face and head. I yelled for the caregivers, and they came running to help me lift her and put her back in her wheelchair. Donna was hurt but didn't scream like she was in much pain. I could see rugburn on her forehead, but she seemed like nothing else was wrong. I let her sit there for a few minutes and then put her on the bed because she was tired. I read to her for a few minutes like I always did at night before she went to sleep. Then I put on a music C.D. for her to listen to so she could fall asleep to it like she always did.

After she went to sleep, I left and, on the way home, prayed God would take her 'home' because I couldn't stand to see her suffer anymore. I felt selfish praying for that, but God showed me something while driving home! I felt the Holy Spirit tell me that Donna was ready to be with the Lord, but He was waiting for me to be prepared for it to happen. I had said it before, but I repeated it. I gave Donna to God and said I was ready to accept her death. I had peace about it and felt it was for her best good. The next day, she woke up okay but ate only a little breakfast and no lunch. The caregivers noticed she seemed like she was going to fall out of her wheelchair; she didn't look good. So, after they put her back to bed, they called me at work and said it was an emergency. Her vital signs were declining. I left my job 5 minutes after I punched in for lunch. Safeway was just 10 minutes from the Home. I wasted no time. When I got to the Ponderosa House, my wife was shutting down, and her vital signs were lowering. I started talking to her and telling her I loved her and was right by her side. I kept saying 'it's me'. I'm right here with you. It's me' is the name she also knows me by, my voice. So, I used to say, "It's me, Cam," but she would repeat, "It's me." I got used to it. She wasn't very responsive, but for almost two hours, I whispered; "I love you, Donna, I love you, Baby; I'm right here by your side, me and you together. I was crying by now. I would tell her Jesus is with you; it's okay if you want to be with Jesus. Finally, the hospice nurse showed up; Donna was starting to come back. The caregivers put the oxygen in her nose, which I think revived and strengthened her. Here is another example of God working. The caregivers were fill-ins for the vacation. They didn't see the Do Not Resuscitate paper pinned to the wall above Donna's bed, or they wouldn't have given her the oxygen. They saved her life. We got her repositioned in bed and changed. We finished talking to the nurse about what to do now, and then Donna fell asleep, so I went home. The next day, as she improved, I went to see her. I leaned over and said in her ear, it's me. She gave me a big smile and laughed. She was happy to see me.

It was April of 2016 when I decided that instead of putting Donna into another home, I would bring her back home with me and take care of her myself. I'd been retired for two years and didn't need the money I made at Love's. I immediately gave my two weeks' notice to Love's and prepared for a new stage of our Alzheimer's Journey. This was almost three years since Donna almost died. Our lives are in God's hands. The average Alzheimer's patient dies around 8-10 years after diagnosis. This was Donna's twelfth year, and she was very much alive. This stage of our journey is what I call the 'Precious Memories' stage. This was the time when worries weren't necessary anymore. Now was the time for laughter. Now was the time for another chance to love my wife in a new way. She was a happy child again. And that's how I saw her, being a child. This freed me up to have fun with her, whether by going for rides or just listening to music; by choosing to bring Donna home, the state gave me extra caregivers to provide me with respite. Our caseworker, Terry, was very happy that I decided to care for Donna again. She said she thought I would make that choice and I did not disappoint her. The other reason Terry was happy is that statistics show that a patient's life is much better if they are in their home.

When my wife came home this time, I decided we would do things together, and she wouldn't always be stuck in the house with a caregiver who was a stranger. Because Donna no longer wore her dentures, she looked like an older woman. Many people who knew her hadn't seen her for a long time. But once our friends got used to seeing Donna that way, they accepted her. It was the same for all the waiters and waitresses who knew Donna. It was hard for them at first, yet they still loved her and were happy to see her out and around. "Stop being embarrassed by your family member with Alzheimer's. This sickness is not a choice." (Author unknown). I used to get upset with the stares we got in public from people. Anyone disabled or sick with dementia and women with bald heads from cancer all get the same look. I've given those looks before myself. Yet now, I was on the receiving side of that behavior. I had to learn two things as my caregiving time went on. Don't take it personally because it's your loved one they are staring at. And two, even more critical, stop being embarrassed.

Donna wasn't responsible for getting Alzheimer's disease. It wasn't like she smoked her whole life and got lung cancer. Just because others couldn't accept or respect her didn't change that she deserved respect. I took her to restaurants with me as long as possible, even though I had to feed her in front of everybody seated near us.

Throughout the years, we would go out to eat in the different restaurants in town. First, it was Denny's because for our budget it was a little cheaper. We got to know the servers who went to work at a different restaurant in Williams after Denny's closed. So, when Donna returned home in 2016, and we started going out again, many of the wait people had already waited on us for years. All these people love Donna and treat her with the utmost respect. Whether it was Pine Country, Jeff's place, Anna's café, or the Red Raven, all had people we knew, and of course, we ran into friends to visit with. Eating out was my hobby. My whole adult life I liked to eat out, to relax and destress. Donna loved the people and would laugh with the children seated near us at other tables.

One of my favorite hobbies was singing karaoke. Donna and I started going to the Canyon Club bar to play pool and have a beer. I think it was in 2010 that Jackie became the night manager/bartender, and she was the one who brought karaoke to the bar. She had a KJ to do the music and she tended the bar. In 2016, my wife was in her 12th year of Alzheimer's, but she still loved to go out and listen to music. No, I didn't say she loved my singing, but she loves listening to the people sing the oldies. Our friend, whom I called Karaoke Ed, whom we met at Miss Kittys in 2006 doing karaoke, would accompany us to Canyon Club. Whenever it was my turn to sing, Edward would sit close to Donna's wheelchair. We weren't worried about her falling out; she had a seatbelt, but if she couldn't hear my voice, she would think she was alone and start to get frightened. Music always made my wife laugh. Her caregivers and I would put music on in the morning when Donna woke up. It soothed and distracted her from any negative hallucinations she might be having.

I had other things going on in my life when my wife came back home. Instead of getting caregivers to sit with her at home, I would bring her with me. I was still in the Toastmasters public speaking group; we met every two weeks. I tried bringing my wife with me a couple of times, but professional people attended these meetings, and she would start laughing when someone was giving a speech. She would laugh at something in her head, but the speaker didn't know that. This happened also when I was filling in for a preacher at a church in Seligman, Arizona. It was a small church, and half the people knew me. Donna would hear my voice and laugh even when I wasn't saying anything. The congregation's people were very gracious and never let Donna's outburst upset them. Nevertheless, after months, I had to give up the preaching position because she couldn't handle the stress of a 100-mile round trip to the church plus sitting for an hour. It's kind of like I was when I was a kid. I couldn't sit still for 5 minutes. I would also take her to the grocery store with me. I would push her wheelchair in front of me with one hand and pull the grocery cart behind us with the other hand.

Donna and I traveled to Tucson while she was home with me. We were blessed to be able to go to my grandson's baby shower for my first great-grandson, Mason. His mother, Tatyana, and father, Brandon, were two proud parents. The second trip we made to Tucson was to see my granddaughter Caitlyn's graduation from the medical course she was taking. That was our last trip together. Donna couldn't mentally or physically handle the anxiety and stress of the 600-mile round trip. It wasn't exactly easy for me, either. At the time, we owned a Jeep Patriot. Donna needed to be changed as we went through Phoenix on our way to Tucson. This I had to do in the backseat of the patriot. The back doors on the jeep were pretty narrow. I couldn't get the wheelchair up close to the back seat. There wasn't room for me and the wheelchair, so I had to lift Donna out of the chair and then turn and lay her on the backseat. Then afterward, lift her and turn her and put her back in the wheelchair, then lift her into the front seat. It was such a hassle that I just did it in the front seat when I changed her on the way home. Not exactly easy to do. It wasn't long after this I bought a Grand Caravan minivan. That way, I could open the whole back end up and lay her down on a comforter. Even still, both trips to see my family were well worth it. And again, it gave me irreplaceable memories.

My subsequent trial in this journey was to last almost three years. I was born in a small village named Edmondville, in Ontario, Canada. My family immigrated to California when I was only nine years old. Since then, as an adult, I had to always carry my immigration card, my 'green card' with me. In 1979, while living in Canada for a short time, I lost my green card and had to get a new one. This new card had no expiration date on it. It was designed to be permanent. That is until the United States was attacked by terrorists on September 11, 2001. After 9-11, the laws changed concerning immigration cards. Now, it is necessary to renew your card every ten years. But I didn't know this. I thought my card was grandfathered in. Well, not exactly true. Before my wife came home, I worked at Love's Truckstop in Williams. During the hiring process, I was told that even though my green card had my picture, it couldn't be used as a legal form of I.D. because it had no expiration date. Okay, wait a minute. Are you saying my immigration card, my green card is no good. I mean, Donna had no problem; she was already a citizen. She was born in Huntington, West Virginia. I didn't know what I was going to do. The political climate leading up to the 2016 presidential elections wasn't going positively for immigrants. And it sure didn't look suitable for illegal immigrants. Suddenly, when Donna came home in April of that year, I had a new anxiety and fear about my legal status and how it could affect her. One night, I had a caregiver come over to sit with Donna so I could go to karaoke with my friend Ed. Usually, it was my habit to buy one mixed drink and sip it for the 2 hours while we were there. We usually arrived around 8 p.m. and usually left around 10 p.m. This worked out because usually, around then, the party crowd would shuffle in, which meant it was time for us to shuffle out. We always got to sing 2 or 3 songs, which was good enough for us. That night, all the way home, I thought about Donna and my green card. What would happen if I got pulled over by a police officer who ran out of compassion and patience for undocumented immigrants whose green cards might not legal? What if this officer was having a bad day and said, 'I'm taking you down to the station for questioning'? "Wait, wait, my wife is at home with a caregiver who has to leave in 15 minutes. My wife has Alzheimer's. She can't be left alone. I didn't know I needed a new card officer. You got to let me go!" I couldn't imagine what would happen to Donna if suddenly I was gone. That didn't happen to me, and the truth is, it probably wouldn't, but that was when I decided to become a United States citizen. As Ed used to tell me, 'I was a man without a country.' I was born Canadian but raised American. It took me over two years to get my citizenship. I would study the constitution and citizenship test questions online at night while Donna watched T.V. or after bed. She didn't live long enough to see my swearing-in ceremony. I realize this wasn't a situation the average caregiver would have to deal with, but one caregivers must be aware of it. What would happen to your patient if you suddenly weren't there, for whatever reason? Fortunately, we never needed to find out.

With Alzheimer's, your memory is slowly taken away, and your speech is snapped right out of your mouth before you can get half a sentence out. But with a sense of humor, it's not something you have to ponder or deliberate on. Without thinking my wife would come back at me with quick remarks like the night I was trying to get her to go to bed. I said you're tired and falling asleep; the proof is in the pudding. Instantly, laughing, she said, "But I don't have any pudding," then rolled over and fell asleep. I could not stop smiling. A week later 'Santa Claus is Coming to Town' was playing on the radio, and I sang to her, "Santa Claus is coming to Town, so you better be good." Without hesitation, she sings back in a little girl's voice "Yes, I will." Of course, it's hard to convey in writing the humor of the moment, but it dawned on me that these moments are for me. I see these memories of her laughter in my heart more and more as time passes. Donna loved to laugh. She would wake up most mornings laughing; when I changed her briefs, she was happy, she would lay there and laugh. One of her favorite television shows was The Bob

Newhart Show. Donna would listen to him every day, just laughing and laughing. She no longer would watch the television; she would listen but knew Bob's voice and would smile immediately. Another was the movie 'Harry the Bunny', for ages 12 months to 4 years old. Donna's laughter, that is what sustained me. Her joyful laughter at watching Harry the Bunny made me laugh. It gave me such joy to see her happy and enjoying her life. Of course, she was a four-year-old kid in her mind. And to me, she was no longer my wife but my child, but that did not matter. We were together again and had a joyous time together for the most part. It wasn't any different, my happiness watching her laugh at cartoons, like Sponge Bob, than it would be watching any four-year-old toddler laughing. You see, I had watched the times of frustration she went through before. I'd shared the confusion when she couldn't understand what was happening to her. I knew firsthand the insanity of Alzheimer's affecting her life. But that time has passed now. Now, the woman was a child. No more frustration, confusion, or insanity, just a child living in a child's world. She watched Harry the Bunny every day along with Bob Newhart and watched cartoons. This was her time of laughter. I used to say she was "babysat" by laughter. I will always cherish the memories I gained by bringing her back home.

From April 2016 to August 2018, Donna was with me at home. It wasn't all fun and laughter. I had help from caregivers most of the time, but in the spring of 2018, I went through a time when I had no caregivers. Two of our regulars had moved on to new jobs. As it turned out, the company that supplied these caregivers was short of workers. They couldn't immediately replace the two caregivers that were helping me. By this time, I was already mentally and physically tired from the long hours I took care of Donna. In April 2018, I called my case worker, Terry, and told her I couldn't do it anymore. I needed to place my wife in a home. I was almost 66 then, and after nearly 14 years of caregiving, I was beat up. Again, I was blessed to find a place in Flagstaff to take Donna. If you've ever been involved in looking for an open bed in a home in most cities, you might be added to an already long waiting list. How fortunate we were that the manager-caregiver, Becky, who also was at the Ponderosa House, had an opening in Rose Arbor, the other Home she took care of. This was now the third and final time I put Donna into a Home, and it wasn't any easier than the first time. By then, she was in a different state of being and didn't put up a fight like the first two Homes. By then, I also knew Becky well enough to know she loved all her patients. We had known each other for five years, so Becky knew Donna's needs. For the first month, I visited Donna twice a day. Finally, Becky convinced me I needed a break, and maybe I should see my family in Southern California. She was right. My wife was in good hands. So, I took a trip to Orange County, California, to see my older brother Colin, and my younger brother Clair, and my younger sister Laurie and their families. I also would visit my dear friends Barry and Fina. Barry and I have been friends since 1965. Even though I only stayed a few days, it was great to see everyone. When I returned from my trip, I was refreshed. I cut back on the 76-mile round trip to see Donna from 2 visits daily to once a day. This would make it much easier and save me gas and time for other things.

One day, it hit me, I have to think of 'my' future. Even though it made me feel guilty, it didn't change the fact that Donna was dying; sometime, she would die. In the fall semester of 2018, I went to Coconino Community College and registered for a Spanish 101 class. I was 66 years old and hadn't been in college since the early 70's. It was in this Spanish class I met Profesora Katie. From the beginning, I was added work for Profesora Katie. For one thing, everyone was online. The students turned their homework in online, checked their grades online, and could chat with the professor online without using her office time. Then there was me. "On-line? What's that, like a party phone line?" I wrote out all my homework by hand and turned it in. I think Professor Katie was 31 years old at the time. She looked at it like, 'What am I supposed to do with this pile of papers?' 'Dude, you been hiding in a cave?' 'Homework is done on the computer?' Profesora Katie tried to teach me 'kindergarten computer,' where to go on the computer for homework, tests, etc. They even had a computer lab where I could get help. I never could figure out how to get the laptop to send the finished paper. Profesora Katie finally said, 'Write it by hand and turn it in. I'll deal with it, which meant now she had to find something to put them in to carry them. I said I write, actually, I print everything. So, when she finally did get around to grading my papers, she had to translate the hieroglyphics to get to the point where she could grade my papers. Profesora Katie had many students, and in this modern world, it was an inconvenience that Profesora Katie never complained about. She gave up many office hours for me and stayed after class many times to help me in areas I was struggling with. By the end of the semester, we became friends. Profesora Katie saw how hard I worked to pass and appreciated my desire to learn Spanish. Many students were just there to fulfill an elective credit. They just wanted to squeak by and pass the class with the least effort. These students have 4 and 5 classes to do homework for, write papers, and attend several times weekly. I'm retired; I enjoyed having only one class twice a week.

Professora Katie also learned about my wife's situation and what I was going through. She encouraged me not to give up on my Spanish throughout the semester. She knew what it meant to me. It was in November of that semester Donna passed away. Profesora Katie called me into her office. Bottom line, she said "I know your wife dying is very hard, and I wouldn't blame you if you quit, but you've worked hard this semester. I would hate to see you lose all you've accomplished. The finals are less than a month away. Don't give up now." I started Spanish after I put Donna in Rose Arbor. I have always wanted to learn to speak Spanish since high school. This was another step in moving on with my life. This was the beginning of accomplishing a lifelong goal, finally! It's because of Profesora Katie I not only succeeded in finishing that semester but have continued with my studies, and we have continued to be friends.

On September 3rd, 2004, when Donna was diagnosed with Alzheimer's, the doctor may as well have said, 'Ma'am, you've been sentenced to death!' There is no cure for Alzheimer's; most people don't see or realize that mourning began when I heard the diagnosis. For many years, in the back of my mind, her death was looming. They say the average patient lives for 8 to 10 years after diagnosis. When that time came, my anxiety rose again, thinking, is this it? Is now the time? One day, I got angry with myself. I'm tired of thinking of Donna's death; she's alive, not dead, and it's time to accept that. I was feeling sorry for myself; she was dying, but I'm feeling sorry for myself! How does that work? Donna knew what was happening to her. One night early on she asked me if she was too much trouble for me and if I wanted to be away from her. I discerned this after a lot of stuttering and broken words. I figured out she felt this way because I had been talking to someone at Hospice Compassus on the phone for the last three days about needing respite. Another time, Donna said she wanted to go home. (To be with the Lord). She was worn out from the struggle. I came home for lunch one day. And she was afraid. I asked her why. It was because the fire had gone out in the woodburning stove, and I was the one who kept it going. Then she asked me if she was going crazy. "Am I too much?" Do you want to be away from me? "Am I going crazy?" "I want to go home." "Are you coming back?" "I want to die!" Can you imagine knowing what you're going through will only worsen, and you don't know if your spouse or family member will stick by you? Your whole life is in someone else's hands. Imagine thinking, will I be too much for them? Maybe it would be better off if I die? She could still think at the time. She still had memory, but now her mind played tricks on her. The hallucinations she had weren't as much visual as mental. Over and over, I reassured her I was there for the long haul. The long haul was getting shorter.

As I said earlier, the mourning period starts before the patient dies. Mourning is in no way unusual for a caregiver of a spouse with Alzheimer's. I got depressed around her 8th year because I thought her time was short. But she lived. In 2013, when she almost died, I went into mourning again. 2017, when she had a seizure in bed, I didn't know if it was her time, yet she recovered. In the winter of 2017 and 2018, Donna went through a period of sleeping 18 hours a day, which I had heard was a sign that the time was near. Again, I slipped into a depression again and again she came out of it. By the time she passed away, I had been mourning the 'death' of my spouse for years. "In the their hearts humans plan their course, but the Lord establishes their steps." (Prov 16:9 NIV) Boy, how that was proven in our journey through Alzheimer's together. It wasn't up to me how long or where she lived. Whenever she was in a different home, we thought it was final. Nothing's final until the Lord says.

"Love is patient, love is kind..." "It is not easily angered; it keeps no record of wrongs." (Ist Corinthians 13) I wasn't this way when I started this journey into Love. I wasn't patient with Donna a lot of the time. My learning period, my training in God's Love, lasted 14 years. It took that long for me to be ready for her to go. Which meant it took me 14 years to learn the lesson of love. I was to learn to love by being my spouse's caregiver and her servant. I knew Donna's love for me didn't go away just because she had Alzheimer's. It increased. In the early years of the journey, there would be times she would grab my face with both hands and tell me she loved me. Her memory of who I was disappeared, but our friendship didn't. We laughed, cried, and got angry many times, yet we never stopped loving each other. It might not make sense that two people could discover God's love by going through Hell. It was humbling for my wife to trust and depend on God and others. This isn't always easy for an independent person. But as long as I knew Donna, she trusted in God. Her faith was always more profound than mine.

Many people realize as they are going through something like this that it's only after going through the experience yourself that you can help others. I began to discover others who had dealt with Alzheimer's, like Valerie, a server at Denny's, who helped take care of her father, who had Alzheimer's. And there was Tara, another server at Denny's whose father-in-law had Parkinson's disease. She and I used to discuss 'end-of-life' decisions. A caregiver must never stop learning from others. I was becoming a better caregiver and a better-qualified person to help others in the future. The 'Love' a person learns through this ordeal won't go away after your patient passes. You learn to love others better, to be patient with others, and always appreciate your daily blessings more deeply. 'Who am I becoming?' takes on a whole new meaning when you take your eyes off yourself and open them up to what you can give to the world around you. 'What do I have to offer others, now?'.

Alzheimers, the Disease   1-25-05
                                           11:08pm

Where in does darkness lie,
But a moment upon your face.
Even then will not the Light shine?
Darkness fading, it has no place.

And fear arising amongst the shadows,
Appearing strong, pathetically weak.
To topple down, a King's Kingdom,
Striking hard, upon His daughter's cheek.

Visibly shaken, her countenance stumbles,
Taken aback, she catches her breath.
Outwardly pausing, returning to Faith.
Folly the moment, this leads not to Death.

Wretched his body, youth has abandoned,
Worn and weary, the days are long.
Forgotten the moments, forgotten the suffering,
Eternity awaits her, filled with song...

Written by Cameron W. Haney

CHAPTER 6

Beyond Death, There Is Life

For the caregiver whose patient dies, your life completely changes. This is your most challenging test of all! Will you choose to move on and live. Or will you choose to die inside? Both of you don't need to pass. All the time I cared for Donna, I read a lot or I practiced singing. My reading focused on what I would like to do in the future. I had three things in mind. One, to finish the book I started years ago. Two, I wanted to be prepared to give 'motivational speeches' to any person or audience at a moment's notice. Three, I wanted to learn Spanish. I couldn't stop Donna's death any more than the doctors could. I became a volunteer caregiver at the home where Donna was. I also became a part-time paid handyperson at the Home. This allowed me to be close to Donna while working and helping out. The other benefit was that it gave me time and something to do while preparing for a new life change. I know you can't change things; that's why you need a short distraction, whether going to coffee with your friends or working part-time. It's not about making money; it's about giving your mind something else to focus on. It burns up anxious and frustrating energy.

Over the years, I've continually read or listened to motivational and self-help books and CDs to keep me going. I got into that habit initially because I wanted to find a way for years to become successful. The key to reading, studying, or learning is, will it uplift and encourage you? Or does it drag you down with guilt over past mistakes and regrets?

I was watching my wife of over 36 years die. At the same time, I was thinking about my future. What will I do? Planning for your future gives you a purpose beyond caregiving, and believing it will happen gives you hope. Each caregiver must see that they will be in a place of freedom. At the moment the patient passes the caregiver is free to choose a new life that works for them. Many have gone before you. There are 11 million examples of unpaid caregivers who are making the same sacrifices you are making and have made right now in America. On the morning of November 8th, I was at the Home with my wife. I leaned over and told her I loved her. She'd been going downhill for the last two weeks. She hadn't moved out of bed in the previous few days. When I had told her I loved her she raised her head up off the pillow and mumbled to me. Then she laid back down. I'd heard of patients having a moment of clarity before they passed. I felt that Donna had that moment and told me she loved me too. The next day, November 9th, 2018, Donna passed away in the morning before I got to the Home. I can't tell you how much that last day we were together, both alive, meant to me. Love to the end. Two days later, I wrote in my journal, "My Dear Woman just graduated with a Master's Degree in Divinity! One with Christ!" All the arrangements for a cremation were set up and paid for. What a relief it was for me not to deal with that then. The Celebration of Life ceremony was a few weeks after she passed. My life just changed forever.

For the first time in years, I was free from Alzheimer's. Donna wasn't suffering anymore; she was with the Lord, and she was free. I know it's hard for some to understand, but I was ready to date soon after she passed; I was finally released from the cage of Alzheimer's. I was prepared for companionship that wasn't just caregiving. For most, they've lost their daily partner and are entirely lost. I went to grief group meetings and had grief counseling. Yet I must say my friends and family got me through. My friend Ellie had lost her husband to Alzheimer's and could relate to what I was going through. We have been friends since 2005, and shared our experience through all the years her husband, Pete, and my wife Donna lived through Alzheimer's. It's hard to express what it means to have a close friend to talk to who knows what you're going through.

Being a caregiver of anyone with dementia is, by definition, a demented life. Your fortitude is tested sometimes several times a day. You cannot fight this fight without depleting your mental and physical strength. Depression comes. And when you're already in a weakened state, it overwhelms you. Make a phone call. You would be helped so much to have someone whose shoulder you can cry on. You need the release of talking to someone. Even when you know it won't change your situation. Just sharing your burden with someone will bring you relief.

Now, we come to the last stage of our Alzheimer's experience—it is time to move on. My wife had moved on; now, it was time for me to move on. The moment Donna passed; my new life began. Over and over, my friends would say, 'That's what she would have wanted.' We are created to live and live to the fullest. It's not required to dwell in the memories constantly to show others how much you loved your spouse. It's not required to carry around a 'guilt,' or I should have, but we do, I do. This is where my support group came in to push me to see it's okay for me to get on with my life. Grieving will be a part of my new life but will become less and less as I open up to new experiences.

I know my caregiver's experience has taken me to Hell and back. And to some, starting over in this world alone is a new kind of Hell. It is my faith in renewal, in God, that has given me the strength to move on. I encourage you to get whatever help you can to help you make it through the before and after life of Alzheimer's. Part of my moving on is writing this book. A few years ago, when they asked what I was doing now, I told everyone in my social circle that I was working on "My Book" again. It would bring closure and would be very therapeutic. The truth is I wasn't writing at all then. I was doing everything I could to avoid writing it. I filled my time with as much 'busy' as I could. It wasn't that I didn't get encouragement from my friends and family telling me of their faith in me. "You can do it." There was something else that was holding me back. My life was going great; I had Denise. I was healthy, and my book had promise. What was it? What kept me in chains., keeping me from fulfilling a whole new purpose in my life? Then it hit me! That 'aha' moment is when you see the absolute truth of what's happening inside. I wanted to move on with my life. I had no desire to relive the pain of the last 14 years of my life with Alzheimer's. Wasn't once enough! Writing this book would cause me to relive it all over again.

I must admit here I never understood why people who had lived through an experience worth writing about sometimes waited years to write their books. I used to think they were doing it for the money, writing this long after it happened. I was wrong. It took these five years to tell the story without breaking down. It took this long to achieve the right mindset to tell my story. It all came down to realizing I could feel sorry for myself or fulfill myself. I want to help people. I want to encourage caregivers that they can survive the experience. The love I've learned through it all has become a part of me now. I'm living proof faith can move mountains. There is life after Alzheimer's. There is hope for the caregiver no matter what your age, I'm 71. Believe in God and believe in yourself. You can accomplish much more than you think you can. Always keep looking forward. Always pick yourself up when you stumble.

My wife deserved the best. She was worth any trouble I might have endured. Because of her and our life together, I am who I am today. Not all I should be, but so much better than I used to be. I thank God for the life we had together. I praised God for the love we shared. I will be forever grateful for the example of Christ's love in action that Donna showed me.

"We don't move on from grief. We move forward with it." This quote came from Nora McInerny when she was giving a Ted Talk. For the first time in 14 years I was free from Alzheimers. Donna wasn't suffering anymore., she was with the Lord. She too was free. For most they've lost their daily partner and are lost. I went to support groups and had grief counseling. This time, just like when I was going through Alzheimers, my friends and family got me through. My friend Ellie, who had lost her husband to Alzheimers 2 years earlier, knew exactly what I was going through. We had been there for each other the whole time. Holding the grief in just extends the pain of your loss. Another person who was there for me was my friend Melissa. Melissa, who I met at the last Home where Donna was, was going through a divorce at the time. We became close friends and used to encourage each other daily through our individual struggles. She was 17 years younger than me and neither one of us was looking for or needed a romantic relationship. That's what made our friendship special at the time. For me to have a female friend and her to have a male friend to talk to without the stress of the dating game. On weekends I would travel to Phoenix where her and her four girls lived. We would all do things together or Melissa and I would go by ourselves and maybe play pool and talk.

At the risk of repeating myself from earlier, I want to say that no matter how much support you've received, you'll never not need encouragement. And now that this life is over it will, again, take all your mental and physical strength to start over. Along with grief there is regrets and guilt that now infiltrate your mind. I was at a point when I needed uplifting the most, I was tearing myself down reliving my regrets and drowning in my own guilt. There came a time when I had to tell myself, just because Donna died, it didn't mean we both had to die.

I wasn't going to get rid of guilt or regrets or grief. I just needed to realize as Miss McInerny said, "We move forward with it."

I've struggled with Depression my whole life, but I know there are ways to overcome it. There are doctors, counselors, pastors, all who can give you help and hope.

When my wife died, I was ready to start a new life. Even with all the friends and family I had I was still lonely.

I was alone, living by myself again. Seven months after Donna died God blessed my life again. I had stayed working at the home where Donna had been as handyman/caregiver. I already had been helping at home while my wife was there for something to do. One day a patient at the Home had a friend come to take her shopping. I recognized the woman as someone who lived in Williams, where I lived. I used to be a meatcutter at the only grocery store in town, Safeway. I recognized her as a customer I had seen in the store. Since I knew the patient, Dolores, I went to her and asked her if she could ask her friend if she would go out with me. Well, it took Denise two months, but she finally said yes. She had asked Dolores about me and had checked out my Facebook page to see what kind of person I was. I'm not sure if it was a moment of weakness or what but she went out with me. We dated for around two or three months when we decided we were in love with each other and wanted to be together. Denise was 59 at the time and I was 68. We've been together ever since. What a blessing she is in my life. I thank God every day for her. I mentioned before my friend Ellie, who lost her husband to Alzheimer's. After Peter died Ellie had decided she would be alone for the rest of her life. She thought she was too old to start over. I mentioned this here because as time went on, Ellie decided she didn't have to be alone for the rest of her life. Even at her age she could start over. At the time she had recently moved to Flagstaff, Arizona. Although online dating wasn't something our generation grew up with. This was the avenue Ellie used to meet people in her age bracket. Being new to the area, she didn't have a church or social group she was involved in to meet new people. After meeting and dating men for a few months Ellie finally found someone whose company she enjoyed and who seemed compatible with her beliefs. Charles is a Christian like Ellie, and both are in their early 80's. It wasn't long before they too fell in love.

I use their example and my example to show ex-caregivers that no matter what your age it's never too late to start over. Ellie and Charles are married now and just like Denise and I they too don't have to spend their later years alone. I'm fully aware that not all people want to start a new life after their spouse has passed. But whether with someone else or alone, you are starting a new life. I only want to encourage you to see that your life isn't over. For me one of my greatest joys is spending time with my grandkids and great-grandsons. I'm able to travel to Tucson three times a year to see them and watch them grow, which I couldn't do before. I'm also able to travel to see my brother and sister in southern California, which I couldn't do before. Also, I was able to travel to Washington state to visit my brother and his wife. If you have family and friends now is the time to get reacquainted with them. Please don't hide away in your house alone with no social activity. That is how depression sets in.

There is no-one in life who doesn't go through trials and tribulations. It's what we do with experience that defines who we are today. Just encouraging someone else is in itself a fulfilling purpose for your new life. I pray and hope I have encouraged you in some way. And if nothing else, I have given you an up-close picture of life with Alzheimer's. Something that will help you understand what your neighbor or friend or relative is going through as a caregiver. Most of all I hope I have encouraged you to embrace your new life with a greater love for yourself and for others. God Bless.

Author Biography

I was a meat cutter for most of my career. I was born in Ontario, Canada. My family moved to Garden Grove, California when I was 9. Sadly, my wife died 3 months before I became a citizen of the United States in January 2019. Of course she wouldn't have understood anyway. I have always enjoyed public speaking and motivating others. It is my desire that I can share my experience as a caregiver with others who are or have gone through the experience of caregiving. My hope is to encourage others to stay strong, to believe in yourselves, and to know God has a purpose for you beyond caregiving. I'm 72 years old and just beginning this new adventure in my life.

Printed in the United States
by Baker & Taylor Publisher Services